ROCKETPREP

I0487462

CISSP Concepts
350 Practice Questions
Dominate Your Certification Exam

Mike Spolsky

Azure Publishing

CONTENT EDITORS: BHAVANI BHARADWAJ, BAISHALI MANDAL

Contents

About The Author

Mike Spolsky has been building secure software systems since 1999. Early in his career, he developed a lightweight encryption algorithm to secure and sign commerce transactions for mobile phones. His current focus is using machine learning to analyze cyberattacks. He is based in New York City.

Outline

Chapter 1 tests your expertise in Identity and Access Management, the domain that focuses on controlling user access to data by understanding access control categories, identification, authentication and authorization, identity as a service, and access control attacks.

Chapter 2 deals with questions related to Communications and Network Security, which covers secure network components and architecture design, network attacks and countermeasures, firewalls, and, intrusion detection and intrusion prevention systems.

Chapter 3 focuses on the foundations of Software Development Security, with questions about security in the software development life cycle, software testing, software, different development models, and security controls in the development environment.

Chapter 4 tests your knowledge in the area of Security and Risk Management, which involves security fundamentals, best practices that support the CIA triad, applying the principles of security governance, qualitative and quantitative risk analysis, and different compliance requirements.

Chapter 5 addresses the area of Security Operations, which includes important operational concepts such as disaster recovery, incident management, logging and monitoring of events, patch and vulnerability management, business continuity planning, and more.

Chapter 6 focuses on questions related to the Asset Security domain, which deals with topics like asset classification, data and system ownership, data handling requirements, data retention, and more.

Chapter 7 covers Security Engineering, which is about applying principles in information systems architecture design using various security models, web and mobile systems and their vulnerabilities, embedded device management, and site and facility design.

Chapter 8 covers Security Assessment and Testing, with questions on topics like security control testing, vulnerabilities in security architecture, strategies for assessment and testing.

1

Identity and Access Management

1. When user identities of two or more unrelated networks are combined without having to synchronize directory information, what is this technique called?

   A. Creeping Privilege

   B. Federation

   C. Access control matrix

   D. Kerberos

2. Which of the following statements is true?

   A. IDAAS are services providing access and identity management functions to specific systems both on a company's physical premises and in the cloud.

   B. IDAAS are services providing hardware and software tools to diverse systems both on a company's physical premises and in the cloud.

   C. IDAAS is a data structure that provides software licensing functions to specific systems both on a

company's offsite premises and in the cloud.

   D. IDAAS are services with fastest OS installation functions both on a physical cloud and a virtual cloud.

3. Which of the following is a type of factor authentication?

   A. Authentication by knowledge

   B. Authentication by skills

   C. Authentication by server

   D. Authentication by tools

4. When an access control method requires the user to use two or more factors, what is this technique called?

   A. Multifactor authentication

   B. Biometrics

   C. Digital signatures

   D. IAM

5. When a security control tool can identify access control vulnerabilities like unnecessary use accounts and can help mitigate them, what is this technique called?

A. Vulnerability Scanner

B. Web Application Scanner

C. Code Scanner

D. Port Scanner

6. When security features are adopted to prevent unauthorized access by limiting a subject's access to an object using access rules, what is this technique called?

A. Formal Verification

B. Access Control

C. User Provisioning

D. Defense-in-depth measures

7. What is the process of periodically checking user accounts to ensure users do not have undue privileges and deactivate dormant accounts called?

A. Access Control

B. User Provisioning

C. Account revocation

D. Account review

8. What is the process of revoking user accounts when an employee is terminated or is on an extended leave of absence to prevent fraudulent activities, called?

A. Account revocation

B. Access Control

C. User Provisioning

D. Account review

9. Which of the following is a Biometric authentication reference factor?

A. Signature dynamics

B. Transponder

C. Smart cards

D. Motion detectors

10. When a system accepts an unauthorized user and grants access by mistake, what is this biometric error called?

A. FCE (Failure to Capture)

B. Error Equal Rate

C. False Acceptance

D. False Rejection

11. When a card has the user's photograph and other identifying information that is worn as a badge and is also used to log on to systems, what is this card called?

A. EAC

B. CAC

C. Proximity Card

D. NIC

12. What is the measure of the accuracy of a biometric system where the false rejection rate is equal to the false acceptance rate, called?

A. CER

B. RE

C. FRR

D. FAR

13. What is the technique of asking questions about predefined responses or facts unique to a specific user that ideally cannot be answered by anyone else, called?

A. Token

B. Single Sign-On

C. Community Strings

D. Cognitive Password

14. What is the access control type where owners of resources are allowed to define and control access to the respective resources based on their discretion called?

    A. Rule-based access control

    B. RBAC

    C. Discretionary Access Control

    D. Mandatory Access Control

15. What is the ratio of Type 2 errors in biometric controls where a system accepts an unauthorized user and grants access by mistake, called?

    A. FRR

    B. CER

    C. RE

    D. FAR

16. What is the ratio of Type 1 errors in biometric controls where a system fails to verify a legitimate user and denies access, called?

    A. FRR

    B. CER

    C. FAR

    D. FER

17. What is the third party ticket authentication system based on symmetric key cryptography where the KDC shares keys with users and services for security, called?

    A. Kerberos

    B. LDAP

    C. SESAME

    D. XACML

18. Which of the following is a component of Kerberos?

    A. LDAP synchronization

    B. Stegomedium

    C. Key Distribution Center (KDC)

    D. Single sign-on

19. What is a hierarchical database model for directory service information on users, clients, and processes provided by network operating systems, called?

    A. NDS

    B. CHAP

    C. LDAP

    D. ADDS

20. Tom is exploring a third-party ticket authentication system based on symmetric key where KDC shares keys with users for security. What technique is Tom using?

    A. XACML

    B. Kerberos

    C. SESAME

    D. LDAP

21. Which of the following is a step in Kerberos logon process?

    A. PAC is created by PAS for user.

    B. Client encrypts username and transmits it to KDC

    C. AS sends token to PAS.

    D. KDC transmits asymmetric key and TGT to client.

22. What is an access control framework where only an authoritative entity like a security administrator can decide and make changes to access levels called?

A. RBAC

B. Mandatory Access Control

C. Non Discretionary Access Control

D. Discretionary Access Control

23. When a biometric identification method uses unique-to-each ridges, creases, and grooves on a palm verify a user's identity, what is this technique called?

A. Hand Geometry

B. Hand Topology

C. Fingerprints

D. Palm scans

24. When a user accumulates too many access rights over time without shedding any old rights, what is this technique called?

A. Privilege creep

B. Kerberos

C. Access control matrix

D. Federation

25. What is the process of determining whether a user (new/existing) is required to have requested access as per the tasks of his role and organizational requirements called?

A. Provisioning process

B. Account revocation

C. Account review

D. Access Control

26. Which of the following is a retinal scanning concern?

A. Retinal scans change during pregnancy.

B. Retinal scans can't identify communicable diseases.

C. Retinal scans can't differentiate twins.

D. Retinal scans reveal low blood pressure.

27. What is an XML based convention that allows exchange of federated authentication and authorization information between security domains over web protocols called?

A. Kerberos

B. SESAME

C. SAML

D. OpenID

28. What is an XML-based lightweight protocol that encodes messages in a web service, decentralized, and distributed environment called?

A. SOA

B. XACML

C. SAML

D. SOAP

29. Which of the following is a type of Single Sign-On?

A. Thick Client

B. RADIUS

C. LDAP

D. SESAME

30. When a KDC component is used as a trusted third party by Kerberos protocol to create tickets for user authentication, what is this technique called?

    A. Ticket Granting Server

    B. AS

    C. TGT

    D. Session Key

31. Which of the following is a type of Non-Discretionary Access Control?

    A. MAC

    B. Rule-based Access Control

    C. Reactive Access Controls

    D. Laissez-faire file sharing

32. Which of the following protocol is covered by the X.500 standards?

    A. SMTP

    B. DISP

    C. ADMD

    D. PRMD

33. What is a non-discretionary access control model that allows users access to resources due to their organizational roles or the tasks assigned to them called?

    A. RBAC

    B. Rule-based access control

    C. MAC

    D. DAC

34. What is a contactless, automatic identification technology that can detect, identify and track people/objects using radio signals and electronic tags, called?

    A. Proximity Cards

    B. RFID

    C. Near Field Communication

    D. Token Devices

Communications and Network Security

1. When a perpetrator seeks to gain illegitimate access to a system by tampering with TCP packets and using falsified identity, what is this technique called?

    A. Sniffer attack

    B. Spoofing attack

    C. Snooping attack

    D. Access aggregation attack

2. What is a network application (application layer, TCP ports 20 and 21) called that allows exchange of files to and from servers which need anonymous authentication?

    A. Telnet

    B. FTP

    C. TFTP

    D. SSH

3. Which of the following best describes a weakness of FTP?

    A. All data is transmitted in plaintext

    B. Does not provide authenticity

    C. Cannot detect spoofed address

    D. Lack of countermeasure

4. What is the terminal emulation network application(TCP port 23) called that allows remote connectivity for command executions but doesn't allow file transfers?

    A. FTP

    B. SSH

    C. TFTP

    D. Telnet

5. Which of the following describes a weakness of Telnet?

    A. No/limited integrity.

    B. No confidentiality: all data including credentials is transmitted in plaintext.

    C. All data is transmitted in plaintext.

    D. No confidentiality.

6. What is the open-community cryptographic protocol that uses port 443, allows interoperability with other technologies and is backward compatible with SSL, called?

  A. TLS

  B. SSL

  C. IPSec

  D. SASL

7. Which of the following describes what TLS can prevent?

  A. Prevents eavesdropping and packet manipulation in VoIP.

  B. Prevents Hacker attacks.

  C. Avoids third-party snooping.

  D. Prevents being an open relay.

8. Which of the following does not describe IPSec?

  A. IPSec is a network protocol that was proposed as a standard by the IETF and allows data communication between network entities.

  B. IPSec extends encryption, authentication of systems, and data integrity.

  C. IPSec is a set of VPN protocol suite that works at the network layer of the OSI model.

  D. IPSec is a standard VPN protocol suite used to secure IP traffic across a network or the Internet via authentication, encryption and hashing.

9. Which of the following is a component of IPSec?

  A. Authentication Header Protocol (For integrity and authentication)

  B. Uses MAC for data integrity.

  C. Session Identity provides a unique session ID to identify and maintain the session as a unit.

  D. Cryptographic keys are used during a session.

10. Which Ethernet Type, has a maximum speed of 100 Mbps, a distance of 100 meters (328 feet), has low difficulty in installation, and a low cost?

  A. 10Base-T

  B. 10Base5

  C. 100Base-T

  D. 1000Base-X

11. Which wireless security standard, is a port-based network access control which provides authentication and key management framework in wireless and wired networks?

  A. EAP

  B. 802.1x

  C. WEP

  D. AES-CCMP

12. What is a sub-protocol of the TCP/IP protocol suite that is used to map IP network addresses to the hardware addresses used by a data link protocol called?

  A. PPP

  B. ARP

  C. RARP

D. SLIP

13. What is the issue caused by an attack responding to ARP broadcast queries to send falsified replies and creation of static ARP entries via ARP command called?

   A. ARP cache poisoning

   B. ARP spoofing

   C. DNS spoofing

   D. DNS cache poisoning

14. Which of the following is a common authentication protocol?

   A. L2TP

   B. PAP

   C. SLIP

   D. IPSec

15. When a hacker gains unauthorized connection through Bluetooth devices to access contact lists, emails, etc. on the target system, what is this technique called?

   A. Bluesnarfing attack

   B. Bluebugging attack

   C. Bluesmacking attack

   D. Bluejacking attack

16. Which of the following is a type of Bluetooth-based attack?

   A. VLAN attack

   B. Warchalking attack

   C. Bluesnarfing attack

   D. Wardriving attack

17. Amy is examining attacks that use Cain and Abel password cracking programs having rainbow tables to recover passwords on Windows. What technique is Amy seeking?

   A. Brute force attack

   B. CAIN attack

   C. ARP Spoofing

   D. Chain attack

18. What is a group of networked systems that compete for the same communication medium and cause a collision if two or more systems transmit at the same time called?

   A. Connection

   B. Collision domain

   C. Polling

   D. Broadcast domain

19. What is a LAN media access technology used in Ethernet networks reacting to collisions and making collision domain members wait before starting processes called?

   A. CSMA/CA

   B. FCoE

   C. DSSS

   D. CSMA/CD

20. When an attacker beats the real replies from a valid DNS server by sending false replies to a requesting system, what is this technique called?

   A. ARP spoofing

   B. DNS Spoofing

   C. IP Spoofing

   D. VLAN attack

21. When an attacker redirects traffic to a malicious system or performs a DoS attack by changing domain-name-to-IP-address mappings, what is this technique called?

    A. ARP spoofing
    B. ARP cache poisoning
    C. DNS Poisoning
    D. DNS Spoofing

22. Which of the following is a security issue for Faxes?

    A. Faxed data can be routed as email to employees.
    B. Faxed data is printed automatically and accessible easily by all.
    C. Faxed data transmitted through Fax servers can be logged and audited.
    D. Faxed data can be based on encrypted transmissions.

23. Which of the following is NOT a security issue for Faxes?

    A. Faxed data is exchanges in cleartext form.
    B. Faxed data transmitted through Fax servers can be logged and audited.
    C. Faxed data is printed automatically and accessible easily by all.
    D. Recorded transmissions can be played back to extract transmitted documents.

24. When traffic is filtered based on the application used to exchange data and the origin of the data using proxy servers are masked, what is this technique called?

    A. Firewall - second generation
    B. Honeypots
    C. Intrusion detection systems
    D. Sandboxing

25. What is a WAN protocol running at data link layer and using packet-switching technology to allow network interfaces to share the same WAN connection called?

    A. LAPB
    B. X.25 network
    C. SMDS
    D. Frame relay

26. Which layer in the OSI model converts bits into electrical signals, and controls electrical, optical and mechanical requirements of data transmission?

    A. Network Layer
    B. Physical Layer
    C. Data-Link Layer
    D. Session Layer

27. Which layer in the OSI model converts data into LAN or WAN frames to allow transmission, defining how a system will access a network?

    A. Session Layer
    B. Data-Link Layer
    C. Network Layer
    D. Application Layer

28. Which layer in the OSI model is concerned with internetworking service, addressing, and routing?

A. Network Layer

B. Session Layer

C. Transport Layer

D. Application Layer

29. Which layer in the OSI model sets up connections between applications, maintains dialog control and negotiates, maintains and takes down communication channels?

   A. Session Layer

   B. Network Layer

   C. Transport Layer

   D. Application Layer

30. Which layer in the OSI model is concerned with compression and decompression of data, encryption and decryption of data, and translations into standard formats?

   A. Application Layer

   B. Session Layer

   C. Presentation Layer

   D. Network Layer

31. Which layer in the OSI model is concerned with file transfer, fulfilling networking requests of applications, network management, and virtual terminals?

   A. Presentation Layer

   B. Application Layer

   C. Session Layer

   D. Network Layer

32. What is a network layer protocol that delivers status and error messages, reports routing information, and helps test connectivity on IP networks, called?

A. RIP

B. ARP

C. BGP

D. ICMP

33. Which of the following is a common Instant Messaging protocol?

   A. IRC

   B. YSMG

   C. Jasper

   D. SOX

34. What is an IP-based SAN protocol that allows linking of data storage facilities, location-independent data storage, transmission and retrieval on Internet called?

   A. iSCSI

   B. MPLS

   C. FCoE

   D. VoIP

35. When a technology breaks telephone lines into channels and allows them to transmit data, voice, and other source traffic digitally, what is this technique called?

   A. SONET

   B. DSL

   C. VPN

   D. ISDN

36. Which of the following does not describe LEAP?

   A. LEAP has significant security flaws.

   B. LEAP is more secure due to encryption.

C. LEAP uses dynamic WEP keys and mutual authentication technique.

D. LEAP is Password based.

37. Which of the following does not describe PEAP?

   A. PEAP is more secure due to encryption.

   B. PEAP uses standard EAP methods within a TLS tunnel.

   C. PEAP is Password based.

   D. PEAP adds encryption to EAP.

38. Which of the following best describes a task group of the 802.11 standards?

   A. 802.11b: 54 mbps, only OFDM

   B. 802.11a: 11 mbps, only DSSS

   C. 802.11n: 1 or 2 mbps

   D. 802.11e: QoS

39. Which of the following best describes a frequency of a task group of the 802.11 standards?

   A. 802.11b: 2.4 GHz

   B. 802.11g: 5 GHz

   C. 802.11n: 5.4 GHz

   D. 802.11a: 2 GHz

40. Which TCP port is used by Microsoft SQL Server?

   A. Port 1521

   B. Port 3389

   C. Port 1443

   D. Port 1720

41. What is an IP address(usually 127.0.0.1) used in machine level self-diagnosis and troubleshooting by creating an interface to connect to itself via TCP/IP called?

   A. RFC 1918 address

   B. Loopback address

   C. Martian address

   D. APIPA address

42. When a factory assigned MAC address of a network interface is changed on a networked device, what is this technique called?

   A. DNS spoofing

   B. ARP spoofing

   C. MAC spoofing

   D. IP spoofing

43. What is a high-throughput networking technology that directs data across a network based on short path labels instead of long network addresses called?

   A. SONET

   B. MPLS

   C. VPN

   D. BGP

44. What is the process of controlling traffic among networked devices by splitting the network into individual network segments, called?

   A. Firmware version control

   B. Security Layers

   C. Application firewalls

   D. Network segmentation

45. Which of the following is a type of Network topology?

   A. Twisted pair Ethernet

   B. RAID

   C. Star

   D. Clustering

46. Which of the following is a layer in the OSI model?

   A. Network Interface

   B. Session Link

   C. Routine

   D. Presentation

47. Which of the following is a security issue for a PBX?

   A. Data is printed automatically and accessible easily by all.

   B. Data is exchanged in clear-text form.

   C. Recorded transmissions can be played back to extract transmitted documents.

   D. Phreakers can hack and alter voice messages leading to brute force and other attacks.

48. What is an attack where a telephone system is hacked using various types of technology and used to make free and/or long-distance calls, steal services, called?

   A. Phishing

   B. Hacktivism

   C. DDoS

   D. Phreaking

49. Which of the following is a tool employed for Phreaking?

   A. Honeypot

   B. Pull boxes

   C. Black boxes

   D. Sandboxes

50. Which protocol provides a graphical interface which enables a computer to connect to another computer over a network connection?

   A. H.323

   B. PPTP

   C. PPP

   D. RDP

51. Which networking device is used to amplify data signals by repeating them between cable segments to physically extend the range of a network?

   A. Gateways

   B. Bridges

   C. Routers

   D. Repeater

52. Which networking device connects similar/different networks by opening data packets, reading network addresses and sending to the right networks?

   A. Gateways

   B. Router

   C. Repeater

   D. Bridges

53. What is a distance vector routing protocol that defines the exchanging of routing table data through routers using hop count as a metric called?

   A. RIP

   B. BGP

C. OSPF

D. IGMP

54. Which of the following statements is true?

A. 802.1x is a wireless security standard that is a port-based network access control which provides authentication and key management framework in wireless and wired networks.

B. EAP is a wired security standard that is a logical access control which provides password policy and cryptanalytic framework in multi-hop networks.

C. 802.1x is a wireless encryption standard that is a type of web control which provides message integrity and information management framework in distributed networks.

D. 802.1x is a wired network standard that is a port-based network access control which provides security and user management framework in wireless and wired networks.

55. Which of the following statements is true?

A. Type of Bluetooth-based attacks are: Blueforce Bluebugging Bluecracking

B. Type of Bluetooth-based attacks are: Bluehacking Bluebugging Blueriding

C. Type of Bluetooth-based attacks are: Bluejacking Bluedriving Bluesnarfing

D. Type of Bluetooth-based attacks are: Bluejacking Bluebugging Bluesnarfing

56. When two/more systems collide by transmitting data at the same time to a connection that only supports a single transmission path, what is the technique called?

A. Polling

B. Collision

C. Broadcast

D. Connection

57. Port 21 is employed by which service?

A. FTPS

B. SSH

C. FTP

D. Telnet

58. Port 25 is used by which service?

A. SSH

B. Telnet

C. FTP

D. SMTP

59. Which service employs Port 80?

A. HTTP

B. HTTPS

C. SSH

D. DHCP

60. Port 123 is employed by which service?

A. IMAP

B. NTP

C. BGP

D. POP

61. Which service employs Port 161/162?

    A. IMAP

    B. POP

    C. SNMP

    D. LDAP

62. 135/UDP server port is employed by which service?

    A. NetBIOS

    B. MS SQL

    C. Active Directory

    D. DHCP

63. When a networking protocol synchronizes clocks of network components with a central clock source to ensure operational stability, what is this protocol called?

    A. NTP

    B. RTP

    C. PTP

    D. SNTP

64. Which of the following is an IP address range outlined in RFC 1918?

    A. 10.0.0.0-10.255.255.255 - 16 Class B ranges

    B. 192.168.0.0-192.168.255.255 - 16 Class B ranges

    C. 10.0.0.0-10.255.255.255 - Class A network

    D. 172.16.0.0-172.31.255.255 - 16 Class A network

65. What is the wireless access protocol that provides 64-bit, 128-bit and 256-bit encryption using the Rivest Ciper4 (RC4) algorithm to protect wireless data called?

    A. WAP

    B. WPA2

    C. WPA

    D. WEP

66. What is the wireless access protocol that addresses the weaknesses of WEP by implementing TKIP, called?

    A. WAP

    B. WEP

    C. WPA

    D. WPA

67. What is the wireless access protocol that provides more secure algorithms by including AES cryptography?

    A. WAP

    B. WPA

    C. WPA2

    D. WEP

68. What is the network discovery scanning technique that sends a packet with all TCP flags (FIN, PSH and URG) set, or lit up like a Christmas tree?

    A. TCP SYN Scanning

    B. TCP Connect Scanning

    C. Xmas scan

    D. Nmap

69. When a VoIP Quality of Service issue occurs due to variation in latency in various packets affecting the quality of conversations, what is the technique called?

    A. Packet Loss

    B. Interference

    C. Latency

D. Jitter

70. Which is the VoIP Quality of Service factor that refers to the time it takes for a packet to travel from a host server to the destination?

A. Interference

B. Packet Loss

C. Latency

D. Jitter

71. What is the cryptographic attack where an attacker maliciously intercepts communication and controls, alters or eliminates the data being exchanged, called?

A. Man in the browser attack

B. Meet in the middle attack

C. Man in the middle attack

D. Rainbow table attack

72. When one or more packets of data are lost between source and destination due to network congestion, what is this technique called?

A. Interference

B. Latency

C. Jitter

D. Packet Loss

73. What is an approach to virtualizing network operation, design, and management, allowing for routing decisions to be made remotely, called?

A. FCoE

B. iSCSI

C. SDN

D. VoIP

74. When a target network is flooded with a series of SYN packets and then ignored by the spoofed source causing it to crash, what is this technique called?

A. Fraggle Attack

B. Ping Flood Attack

C. Smurf Attack

D. SYN Flood Attack

75. When a target system is flooded with numerous spoofed ping requests, leaving it with no time to respond to legitimate requests, what is this technique called?

A. Fraggle Attack

B. SYN Flood Attack

C. Ping Flood Attack

D. Smurf Attack

76. When spoofed broadcast/echo ICMP packets are sent to a target system's network broadcast address drawing traffic on the network, what is the technique called?

A. SYN Flood Attack

B. Ping Flood Attack

C. Fraggle Attack

D. Smurf Attack

77. When UDP packets with spoofed IP address of a victim are sent to a target system's network broadcast address attracting traffic, what is this technique called?

A. SYN Flood Attack

B. Ping Flood Attack

C. Smurf Attack

D. Fraggle Attack

78. When a network device limits access from one network to another, internally and externally, and filters malicious internet traffic, what is this technique called?

A. Firewall

B. PAP

C. Intrusion detection system

D. Honeypot

79. Which of the following filtering rule can be used to prevent IP spoofing?

A. Allow direct IP user authentication.

B. Packets with internal source IP addresses don't enter the network.

C. Packets with public IP addresses would not pass through routers in either direction.

D. Avoid use of cryptographic protocols to authenticate packets.

80. When a hybrid vulnerability scanning tool is used to scan both the network and the web for vulnerabilities, what is this tool called?

A. Metasploit

B. Nmap

C. Snort

D. Nessus

81. When a network discovery scanning tool is used to check the state of network ports and discover hosts and services to create a map of it, what is this tool called?

A. Nmap

B. Snort

C. Metasploit

D. Nessus

Software Development Security

1. What are shortcuts installed by programmers called to bypass system checks during development that become security threats if not removed before the release?

   A. Maintenance hook

   B. Temporal isolation

   C. TOC/TOU

   D. Race conditions

2. When an attacker with limited access manages to gain access to additional resources beyond his access rights, what is this technique called?

   A. Brute force password guessing

   B. SQL Injection

   C. Vertical escalation

   D. Privilege escalation

3. Which of the following can be classified as a Programming Language generation?

   A. Natural Language

   B. Machine Code

   C. Expert Language

   D. 6GL

4. Which of the following is NOT a type of Programming Language Generations?

   A. Machine language

   B. Natural language

   C. Compiled Language

   D. Expert Language

5. Which of the following is a type of ACID integrity components?

   A. Atomicity

   B. Rationality

   C. Authenticity

   D. Interoperability

6. When pieces of less sensitive information are combined to provide new information of a higher sensitivity level beyond the user's access rights, what is this concept called?

   A. Compilation functions

   B. Joining functions

   C. Union functions

D. Aggregating functions

7. When software is developed using an interactive and incremental development model that encourages flexibility, adaptability and team collaboration, what is this process called?

   A. Cleanroom Model

   B. Spiral Software Development Model

   C. CASE

   D. Agile

8. Which of the following is a type of Artificial Intelligence systems?

   A. Expert Systems

   B. OLAP

   C. Management Information Systems

   D. Transaction Processing Systems

9. When an interaction between a web application and another application/OS/database is allowed, what is the technique called and what is the code that acts as passwords on function calls called?

   A. Plugin

   B. Create ActiveX

   C. DCOM

   D. API and API Keys

10. When a network of several systems stands compromised with zombie codes, and is used to send spam/phishing emails, what is the technique called?

    A. Adware

    B. Spyware

    C. Botnet

    D. List Poisoning

11. When a variable is checked if it is within specified limits or constraints before it is used, what is this method called?

    A. Consistency Check

    B. Data Validation

    C. Bounds Checking

    D. Length Checking

12. When an attacker seeks to flood a system with more data than the buffer allows and thus causing system failure or compromise, what is this method called?

    A. Shellcode

    B. Heap Overflow

    C. Buffer Overflow

    D. Buffer over-read

13. When software tools like program editors, code analyzers, etc. are used in automated development and maintenance of software, what is this technique called?

    A. Structured Development Model

    B. Agile Software Development

    C. CASE

    D. Sashimi Software Development Model

14. When the changes that occur during any phase of a system life cycle are controlled and the change control activities are documented, what is this process called?

A. Software Escrow

B. Capability Maturity Model Integration (CMMI)

C. Changelog

D. Change Control

15. Which of the following is a stage in the Change Control process?

   A. Software Development

   B. Change request

   C. Optimizing process improvement

   D. Prototyping

16. While developing a product when the focus is on defect prevention that is achieved by structured methods during developing and testing, what is this model called?

   A. Agile

   B. Joint Analysis Development (JAD)

   C. Reuse model

   D. Cleanroom

17. When the ability of a program to perform different types of tasks independently without interacting with any other programs is measured, what is this technique called?

   A. Code Review

   B. Cohesion

   C. Coupling

   D. Data Modeling

18. When a perpetrator attacks through unauthorized commands that are executed in an OS through a vulnerable application, what is this technique called?

A. Buffer Overflow

B. Spoofing

C. Command Injection

D. Malware

19. When a program converts high-level source code into an executable binary file targeted for a specific OS, what is this language called?

   A. Compiled Language

   B. Procedural Language

   C. Assembly Language

   D. Interpreted Language

20. When a program executes instructions without previously compiling into machine language, but is prone to malicious code insertion, what is this language called?

   A. Interpreted Language

   B. Procedural Language

   C. Assembly Language

   D. Compiled Language

21. When a process ensures that the changes made to software versions are in line with the change control and configuration management requirements, what is this technique called?

   A. Configuration Status Accounting

   B. Configuration Control

   C. Configuration Audit

   D. Configuration Identification

22. Which of the following is a stage in the Configuration Management process?

A. Configuration Initiating

B. Release Control

C. Configuration Status Accounting

D. Change Control

23. When the level of interaction a module needs to make with other programs to carry out its tasks is measured, what is this technique called?

A. Cohesion

B. Coupling

C. Code Review

D. Data Modeling

24. When a web attack uses 3rd party redirect of static connect within the security context of a trusted site, what is this technique called?

A. XSS

B. Injection

C. Security Misconfiguration

D. CSRF

25. When a database for system developers records all data structures used by a particular application including sources, type, etc., what is this technique called?

A. Schema

B. Data Dictionary

C. Record

D. View

26. When multiple users or applications try to extract data concurrently and some preventive controls maintain the integrity of data, what is this technique called?

A. Perturbation

B. Database Concurrency

C. Cell Suppression

D. Partitioning

27. When discrete sets of SQL instructions are used by relational databases to ensure data security, what is this technique called?

A. Database transactions

B. Data analytics

C. Database shadowing

D. Remote Journaling

28. When a development approach is adopted focusing on three elements- software development, quality assurance and IT operations, what is this approach called?

A. IDEAL model

B. Spiral

C. DevOps

D. Sashimi

29. When an attacker seeks to traverse inaccessible directories by inserting the characters "../" many times into the URL, what is this technique called?

A. CSRF

B. SQL Injection

C. Directory traversal attack

D. Buffer Overflow

30. When vulnerabilities of a software is publicly disclosed by its researchers without any restrictions, what is this approach called?

A. Compromise

B. Inadvertent Disclosure

C. Full Disclosure

D. Partial Disclosure

31. Which of the following is a way to protect against a SQL Injection attack?

A. Encryption

B. User authentication

C. Using triggers

D. Limiting account privileges

32. Which of the following is a phase of the IDEAL software development model?

A. Repeatable

B. Optimizing

C. Acting

D. Defined

33. When a user deduces information that is not explicitly available, what is this technique called?

A. Inference

B. Data Analytics

C. Warehousing

D. Aggregation

34. When a user has access to particular information and is able to deduce information that she is not authorized to access, what is this attack called?

A. Polyinstantiation

B. Aggregation

C. Inference attack

D. Perturbation

35. When security characteristics of the main class (super/parent class) are inherited automatically by subclasses, what is this technique called?

A. Encapsulation

B. Polymorphism

C. Polyinstantiation

D. Inheritance

36. When a platform independent virus, written in Word Basic, Visual Basic or VBScript macro languages, infects documents and templates, what is this virus called?

A. Compression virus

B. Polymorphic virus

C. Stealth virus

D. Macro virus

37. Which of the following is a type of a Malware?

A. DoS

B. Logic Bombs

C. Injection

D. Buffer overflow

38. Which of the following is a Malware detection technique?

A. Intrusion detection system

B. Passive infrared system (PIR)

C. Known Signature Scanning

D. Content filtering

39. When bootable media portions (single disk sectors) are used by a computer to load an operating system during the boot process, what is this technique called?

A. Master boot record

B. Boot sector

C. System boot record

D. Boot loader

40. When a virus attacks the MBR by redirecting system to infected boot sector loading the virus before the OS during the boot process, what is this virus called?

A. Service Injection Virus

B. File Infector Virus

C. MBR Virus

D. Macro Virus

41. When a programming language model is organized around self-sufficient reusable objects that combine methods and data, what is this model called?

A. OOD

B. OORA

C. OOP

D. OOA

42. When the source code of a software program is made available to anyone, what is this approach called?

A. Open Source

B. Close Source

C. Freeware

D. Public domain software

43. What is OWASP?

A. OWASP is designed as a standard to encode documents and data.

B. OWASP is an open non-profit project which helps improve the security of web-based application software and free sharing of methodologies and techniques in the area.

C. OWASP is a non-profit project that allows multiple applications to be consumers of services and reduces application architecture to a unit of functionality.

D. OWASP is a convention for the organization and an open-standard data format used for exchanging authentication and authorization of data.

44. When security vulnerabilities of a software/hardware are disclosed to the vendor, giving a chance to fix flaws and release a patch, what is this approach called?

A. Full Disclosure

B. Compromise

C. Partial Disclosure

D. Inadvertent Disclosure

45. When a preventive measure against password-cracking is adopted along with a set of rules for users to create strong passwords, what is this technique called?

A. IAM preventive and detective controls

B. Multifactor authentication

C. Account Lockout Controls

D. Password policy

Security and Risk Management

1. What is the value that denotes the predicted frequency of a particular risk which is realized within a year called?

   A. AF

   B. ARO

   C. ALE

   D. AV

2. Which of the following is a phase of the BCP?

   A. Identify critical business functions of a company

   B. Risk determination

   C. Threat Identification

   D. Continuity Planning

3. Which of the following is stage in the BCP?

   A. Threat Identification

   B. Identify critical business functions of a company

   C. BCP training

   D. Risk determination

4. Which law mandates all communications service providers to make wiretap option available for law enforcement agencies irrespective of the technology used?

   A. ECPA

   B. CALEA

   C. HITECH

   D. CCCA

5. When an alternate control providing the same level of security as the original one is chosen due to cost/business requirements, what is this technique called?

   A. Deterrent Control

   B. Corrective Control

   C. Compensating Control

   D. Recovery Control

6. Which law regulates the collection of information from children by websites, and mandates sites to provide privacy notice and operator contact details?

A. SOX

B. FERPA

C. COPPA Act

D. GLBA

7. When an assignable legal right protects an author's work from unauthorized duplication, what is this technique called?

A. Patent

B. Trademark

C. Copyright

D. Trade Secret

8. When a perpetrator prevents authorized users from accessing resources by malicious traffic flooding or exploiting design flaws, what is this technique called?

A. Spoofing

B. Buffer Overflow

C. Denial of service (DoS)

D. War Dialing

9. When post facto access controls are deployed to detect the activities of an unauthorized incident and to identify intruders, what is this technique called?

A. Compensating Controls

B. Deterrent Controls

C. Detective controls

D. Preventive controls

10. Luke wants to adopt access control measures that discourage intruders from attacking or warm them not to attack. What technique should Luke use?

A. Detective controls

B. Deterrent Controls

C. Corrective Controls

D. Preventive controls

11. When an entity uses reasonable care, prudent management, and common sense to protect its interests, what is this technique called?

A. Due Diligence

B. Compliance

C. Asset Protection

D. Due Care

12. Which law penalizes the theft of trade secrets from U.S. corporations or government agencies with or without intending to benefit a foreign government?

A. Economic Espionage Act

B. UCITA

C. DMCA

D. Electronic Communications Privacy Act

13. Which law protects individuals against unlawful monitoring or disclosure of electronic communication including voicemails, emails, and mobile phone calls?

A. CALEA

B. ECPA

C. HITECH

D. CCCA

14. Which US law allows financial institutions like banks and insurance companies to provide a variety of services and share customer information among themselves?

A. HIPAA

B. Gramm Leach Bliley Act

C. Sarbanes-Oxley Act (SOX)

D. FISMA

15. When an unauthorized user takes advantage of a system design vulnerability to access private, confidential or controlled information, what is the attack called?

    A. Repudiation

    B. Denial of Service (DoS)

    C. Information disclosure

    D. Elevation of privilege

16. What is the security standard that defines the requirements for the establishment, control, and implementation of an information security management system?

    A. ISO 27001

    B. ISO 27000

    C. ISO 27002

    D. ISO 27005

17. When a security standard outlines the code of practice for information security management, what is this standard called?

    A. ISO 27002

    B. ISO 27001

    C. ISO 27005

    D. BS 7799

18. What is the technique that defines the maximum period of downtime that can be endured by a business function before any irreversible damage is caused?

    A. WRT

B. MTD

C. RTO

D. MTO

19. Which of the following is a stage of the NIST SP800-34?

    A. Repeatable

    B. Labeled security

    C. Performing Business Impact Analysis

    D. Controlled access protection

20. When access control mechanisms are stationed to protect systems, personnel, and other resources within a facility, what is this technique called?

    A. Physical Controls

    B. Operational Controls

    C. Soft Controls

    D. Logical Controls

21. When proactive control systems are adopted to keep unauthorized activities from occurring in the first place, what is this technique called?

    A. Compensating Controls

    B. Detective controls

    C. Deterrent Controls

    D. Preventive controls

22. When a part of the federal sentencing guidelines calls for executives to take ownership of processes as prudent persons would do, what is this approach called?

    A. Computer Security Act (CSA)

    B. GISRA

    C. Prudent man rule

D. Federal Information Security Management Act

23. When a subjective method of assessing risk is used by ranking threat scenarios instead of calculating monetary figures of losses, what is this technique called?

    A. Quantitative Risk Assessment

    B. Hybrid Risk Assessment

    C. Qualitative Risk Assessment

    D. Target Risk Assessment

24. Which of the following is a step of Quantitative risk analysis?

    A. Calculate ARO

    B. Create scenarios

    C. Structured walkthrough

    D. Use Delphi Technique

25. When countermeasures are implemented to reduce risk levels, to block threats and remove weaknesses, what is this process called?

    A. Risk acceptance

    B. Risk assessment

    C. Risk avoidance

    D. Risk Mitigation

26. When risks and any costs of losses are shifted from one party to another, what is this strategy called?

    A. Risk acceptance

    B. Risk avoidance

    C. Risk Transference

    D. Risk Mitigation

27. What is the metric used in disaster recovery that defines the acceptable amount of data loss, measured in time?

    A. RPO

    B. MTO

    C. RTO

    D. MTD

28. When a perpetrator gains illegitimate access to a system by tampering with the TCP packets and using falsified identity, what is this technique called?

    A. Probing

    B. Snooping

    C. Spoofing

    D. Piggy backing

29. Which of the following is not a step of the Business Impact Analysis?

    A. Make a formal request for change.

    B. Calculate the risk for each business function.

    C. Select people for data gathering.

    D. Identify company's critical business functions.

30. When a perpetrator attacks to alter, falsify or manipulate data without authorization while in storage or transit, what is this technique called?

    A. Impersonation

    B. Repudiation

    C. Tampering

    D. Spoofing

31. What is the critical intellectual property of a company which, if made public could harm the company's profitability and survival?

    A. Patent
    B. Trade Secret
    C. Copyright
    D. Trademark

32. What is the technique that protects certain words, symbols, slogans, and logos that represent a company, its brands, and its products or services called?

    A. Patent
    B. Trade Secret
    C. Trademark
    D. Copyright

33. What is the security tool that is used to identify weaknesses against potential threats in the systems as well as control mechanisms of an organization?

    A. Vulnerability Assessment
    B. BIA
    C. MTD
    D. Risk Assessment

34. Who is the person that is responsible for creating the information security program and appropriately funding, staffing and has organizational priority?

    A. Classification Administrator
    B. Business Owner
    C. Classification System Owner
    D. Data processor

35. What is the regulation passed by the European Parliament intending to strengthen protection of personal data for individuals within the European Union, called?

    A. EU GDPR
    B. EU Data Protection
    C. EU Copyright Directive
    D. EU Privacy Principles

36. Which US law binds all federal agencies, government contractors, and vendors to have information security programs to protect federal information systems?

    A. GLBA
    B. NIIPA
    C. CSA
    D. FISMA

37. What is the preventive access control method which can prevent fraud by making it impossible for only one individual to access sensitive resources?

    A. Due Diligence
    B. Social Engineering
    C. Rotation Of Duties
    D. Separation Of Duties

38. What is the framework of IT security best practices that recommend security control requirements, ensuring IT security is aligned with company's goals called?

    A. ITIL
    B. SABSA
    C. NIST 800-53
    D. COBIT

39. Which of the following best describes the ISC2 code of ethics?

    A. Respect privacy and confidentiality.
    B. The practice of ethical code.
    C. Observance of high standard of skill.
    D. Protect society, the commonwealth, and the infrastructure.

40. When a security principle allows authorized users timely and uninterrupted access to resources, what is this technique called?

    A. Availability
    B. Identification
    C. Authorization
    D. Integrity

41. What is the security principle that ensures secrecy of objects, data, and resources and protects them against unauthorized disclosure, called?

    A. Confidentiality
    B. Integrity
    C. Reliability
    D. Availability

42. What is the security principle that assures the accuracy of resources by eliminating risks of unauthorized modification, called?

    A. Availability
    B. Identification
    C. Integrity
    D. Authorization

43. When an attacker tricks users into disclosing sensitive information through emails or links to websites that look legitimate, what is this technique called?

    A. Vishing
    B. Phishing
    C. Social Engineering
    D. Pharming

44. Which of the following is a stage in penetration testing methodology?

    A. Reconnaissance
    B. Threat Identification
    C. Risk determination
    D. Identify critical business functions of a company

45. What is a threat modeling tool that graphically represents all the ways in which specific threats can be realized, called?

    A. Fault tree
    B. Threat tree
    C. Call tree
    D. Spanning tree analysis

5

Security Operations

1. What is an alternate processing site equipped for emergencies with basic environmental and electrical support, but no computing facilities called?

   A. Cold site

   B. Tertiary Site

   C. Warm Site

   D. Hot Site

2. What is an alternate processing site having basic infrastructure and a few extra facilities like HVAC, but not any communication or computing systems, called?

   A. Cold site

   B. Warm Site

   C. Tertiary Site

   D. Hot Site

3. What is a fully configured backup facility equipped with communications links, server, and workstations that can be operational in just a few hours called?

   A. Warm Site

   B. Cold site

   C. Hot Site

   D. Tertiary Site

4. When a reciprocal agreement binds two organizations to help each other in case of emergency situations, what is this technique called?

   A. EULAs

   B. Opt-in agreement

   C. Information security management agreement

   D. Mutual aid agreement

5. What is a suite of technologies that can detect and block data exfiltration attempts by scanning keywords preventing loss of sensitive information, called?

   A. IPS

   B. DLP system

   C. Egress Monitoring

   D. Watermarking

6. What is a high volume electronic mailing list that discusses computer security issues covering vulnerabilities, methods of exploitation, solutions, etc. called?

   A. CVE

   B. Bugtraq

   C. Honeypot

   D. Security Basics

7. What is a suite of security solutions that detect and block data exfiltration attempts by scanning data, looking for data patterns and keywords, called?

   A. Egress Monitoring

   B. IDS

   C. IPS

   D. DLP

8. Which of the following is a step in the Disaster recovery process?

   A. Proactive testing

   B. Assess Damage

   C. Vendor lock-in deployed

   D. Staffing for Resilience

9. Which of the following best describes a type of trusted recovery?

   A. Trusted recovery performed manually by an administrator after a crash.

   B. Automated recovery includes design and audit records.

   C. Trusted recovery implements DAC.

   D. Trusted recovery implements MAC.

10. Which of the following is a physical control?

    A. Server Images

    B. Monitoring and supervising

    C. Mantrap

    D. ACL

11. What is a physical control in the form of an entry gate called that prevents tailgating by allowing only one person in one direction per authentication?

    A. Alarm system

    B. Mantrap

    C. Turnstile

    D. Motion Detectors

12. What is an intrusion detection control that senses and uses movement to identify presence in a controlled area, called?

    A. Mantrap

    B. Turnstile

    C. Alarm system

    D. Motion detector

13. What is the control mechanism that triggers a notification to alert responders in case of an intrusion called?

    A. Mantrap

    B. Turnstile

    C. Alarm system

    D. Motion detector

14. What is a visual recording device called that transmits videos to screens monitored by the security personnel to the detect presence of intruders?

    A. Turnstile

B. Motion detector

C. Mantrap

D. CCTV camera

15. Which motion detector is designed to detect meaningful changes in the infrared lighting pattern of a given area?

A. Capacitance motion detector

B. Wave pattern motion detector

C. Infrared motion detector

D. Heat-based motion detector

16. Which of the following is a RAID level?

A. Tertiary parity data

B. Macro-level parity

C. Unit level parity

D. Interleave parity

17. What is the team responsible for identifying, monitoring, and responding to computer security incidents in an organization, called?

A. CSIRT

B. CVE

C. CERT

D. Bugtraq

18. What is the unused portion of a network's allocated IP addresses, called?

A. F2F

B. VPN

C. Darknet

D. Sneakernet

19. What is the type of database backup where the remote server is updated with copies of database modifications in real-time as they are to the production server?

A. Remote journaling

B. Remote Mirroring

C. Electronic Vaulting

D. Tape Vaulting

20. What is the type of database recovery where actual files are copied as they are modified and periodically transferred to an offsite facility called?

A. Electronic Vaulting

B. Remote Mirroring

C. Tape Vaulting

D. Remote journaling

21. What is a method of data backup where data is backed up on tapes and transferred either manually or electronically to an offsite facility called?

A. Tape Vaulting

B. Remote Mirroring

C. Remote journaling

D. Electronic Vaulting

22. When a replication happens in real-time across repositories, what is this technique called?

A. Synchronous Replication

B. Semi-Synchronous Replication

C. Asynchronous Replication

D. Point-in Replication

23. When a system continues to operate despite suffering a single component fault, what is this technique called?

    A. Failover

    B. RPO

    C. Fault Tolerance

    D. Redundancy

24. What is a type of intrusion detection system that is installed on a host computer to monitor anomalous activity and report it to the administrator, called?

    A. Application Whitelisting

    B. HIPS

    C. HIDS

    D. Perimeter Firewall

25. What is a pseudo flawed system set-up like a genuine system on a network with valid resources to lure intruders and keep them away from the live network called?

    A. IDS

    B. Honeynet systems

    C. Honeypot systems

    D. Sandboxing

26. What is the process of detecting an issue, finding its cause, minimizing the damage, resolving the issue, and documenting these response steps, called?

    A. COOP

    B. User Entitlement Audit

    C. Incident Management

    D. Incident Response

27. Which of the following is a step in the Incident response process?

    A. Business impact assessment

    B. Remediation

    C. Reconnaissance

    D. Enumeration/Scanning

28. When a document records the intention of two parties to work together to achieve a common goal, what is this method called?

    A. Community Cloud

    B. OLA

    C. SLA

    D. MOU

29. When an administrative control principle allows users access only to resources that they need to perform their jobs, what is this method called?

    A. Least Privilege

    B. Separation of duties

    C. Need to Know

    D. Authorization Creep

30. What is an agreement between two departments of an organization describing the level of service expected, service measurement metrics, penalties, etc. called?

    A. Community Cloud

    B. OLA

    C. SLA

    D. MOU

31. Which of the following is a requirement for any evidence to be admissible in court?

    A. Hearsay

B. Peripherality

C. Redundant

D. Properly Identified

32. When administrators assign rights to users depending on the type of privileged operation instead of granting unrestricted access, what is this technique called?

A. Two-person control

B. Job Rotation

C. Segregation of Duties

D. Separation of privileges

33. What are a suite of updates, enhancements or fixes to a software delivered to the user as a single installable package, called?

A. Patches

B. Hot Fix

C. Service Pack

D. Bug Fix

34. What is a project management document that describes the product and customer requirements and defines deliverables, project-specific activities and timelines called?

A. WBS

B. SOW

C. PWS

D. SOO

35. Which of the following statements is true?

A. Database recovery and its types are: Remote Mirroring Transaction Logging Electronic Vaulting

B. Disaster recovery and its types are: Remote Mirroring Remote Journaling Electronic Vaulting

C. Database recovery and its types are: Remote Mirroring Remote Journaling Electronic Vaulting

D. Database recovery and its types are: Remote Mirroring Fault Recovery Media Management

36. Which of the following statements is true?

A. Asynchronous Replication is a replication that happens in real-time across repositories.

B. Synchronous Replication is a replication that uses periodic snapshots of the real-time across repositories.

C. Synchronous Replication is a replication that happens in real-time across repositories.

D. Synchronous Replication is a replication that does not happen in real-time and also offers no durability.

37. When a system recovers after failure in an open state providing all access, what is this technique called?

A. Fail-closed state

B. Fail-open state

C. Fail soft

D. Fail-secure state

38. When a primary system fails or goes offline and a critical fault-tolerant function makes a

standby system available automatically, what is this technique called?

A. Fail soft

B. Failback

C. Failover

D. Fail-secure

39. When a system not only detects but is also equipped to block attacks to a target system before they occur, what is this technique called?

A. Firewalls

B. Antimalware

C. Intrusion detection systems

D. Intrusion prevention systems

Asset Security

1. When regulations by US DoC are adopted to prevent unauthorized cross-border data disclosure, what is this policy called?

   A. EU safe harbor privacy principles

   B. OECD principles

   C. Sarbanes-Oxley Act

   D. US Privacy Act of 1974

2. Which of the following is a standard metric for the Application Security business function of the CIS Security Benchmark?

   A. Risk assessment coverage

   B. Mean-time to complete changes

   C. Mean-time to incident discovery and recovery

   D. InfoSec budget as percentage of IT budget

3. Which of the following is a standard metric for the Configuration Change Management business function of the CIS Security Benchmark?

   A. Risk assessment coverage

   B. Mean-time to complete changes

   C. InfoSec budget as percentage of IT budget

   D. Mean-time to incident discovery and recovery

4. Which of the following is a standard metric for the Financial Management business function of the CIS Security Benchmark?

   A. Percent of changes with security review

   B. Mean-time to complete changes

   C. InfoSec budget as percentage of IT budget

   D. Mean-time to incident discovery and recovery

5. Which of the following is a standard metric for the Incident Management business function of the CIS Security Benchmark?

   A. InfoSec budget as percentage of IT budget

B. Percent of changes with security review

C. Mean-time to complete changes

D. Detection by internal controls (

6. Which of the following is a standard metric for the Patch Management business function of the CIS Security Benchmark?

A. Mean-time to incident discovery and recovery

B. Mean-time to patch

C. Mean-time between incidents

D. Mean-time to complete changes

7. Which of the following is a standard metric for the Vulnerability Management business function of the CIS Security Benchmark?

A. Mean-time to complete changes

B. Mean-time between incidents

C. Mean-time to patch

D. Vulnerability scan coverage

8. Who is the person responsible for creating and assigning rights to user accounts as per classification rules and access control policies?

A. Business Owner

B. Classification System Owner

C. Classification User

D. Classification Administrator

9. Who is the person responsible for the actual system that houses and/or processes sensitive data and is responsible for the security of the data during processing?

A. Business Owner

B. Classification User

C. Classification Administrator

D. Classification System Owner

10. Who is the person who routinely accesses data through a computing system for work-related tasks?

A. Classification System Owner

B. Business Owner

C. Classification Administrator

D. Classification User

11. What is the label for the data ordered above the unclassified level in the US military data classification and exempt from laws like the Freedom of Information Act?

A. Private

B. Declassified

C. Unclassified

D. Classified

12. What is the label for the highest level of classification of data in commercial businesses which means the data is most sensitive and for internal use only?

A. Private

B. Sensitive

C. Confidential

D. Public

13. When the protection of data is achieved through whole-disk, database, PGP, or other kinds of software-based encryption programs, what is this technique called?

    A. Data in Use

    B. Data at rest protection

    C. Data in Flight

    D. Data in transit protection

14. What is the data classification label where the data should stay internal to the business and any infringement could cause grave damage to the organization?

    A. Sensitive

    B. Confidential

    C. Public

    D. Private

15. When data protection is achieved through transport encryption protocols like IPSec, SSL, and SSH, what is this technique called?

    A. Data at Rest

    B. Data in Transit

    C. Data in Flight

    D. Data in Use

16. When data is placed in temporary storage buffers while being used by an application, what is this technique called?

    A. Data at rest

    B. Data in Use

    C. Data in Flight

D. Data in transit

17. What is the data classification process called, where labels are assigned to electronic data, or physically marked in the case of data objects?

    A. Data Storage

    B. Data labeling

    C. Data Handling

    D. Data Sanitization

18. Which of the following is a government regulated method for Data privacy protection in the US?

    A. Encryption

    B. GLBA

    C. PCI DSS

    D. Awareness to Increased Security

19. Who is the person or entity, usually a third party vendor, that processes personal data on behalf of a data controller?

    A. Classification System Owner

    B. Business Owner

    C. Classification Administrator

    D. Data processor

20. What is the residual magnetic flux called that remains on the hard drive as a physical representation of the data after erasure?

    A. Data processor

    B. Data labeling

    C. Data sanitization

    D. Data remanence

21. What is the destruction of data from a system using a trusted method, which could be a combination of processes, to make sure it cannot be recovered, called?

    A. Data remanence
    B. Data sanitization
    C. Data labeling
    D. Data processor

22. What is the process of removing or reducing the security classification on a media or a system called, in order to reuse it in an unclassified environment?

    A. Unclassified
    B. Classified
    C. Declassification
    D. Private

23. Which of the following is a EU Data Protection principle?

    A. Structured processes are carried out for high-level security compliances.
    B. Shall identify company assets to be assessed.
    C. Shall be dealt with appropriate measures to protect against accidental loss or damage.
    D. Shall take corrective and preventive actions based on ISMS audit.

24. What is the technology called that provides superior security that partial encryption like encryption of files/folders by encrypting the data on the disk?

    A. Digital Rights Management
    B. Digital Forensics
    C. Single Sign-On
    D. Full disk encryption

25. What is a cryptographic feature on Microsoft Windows called that offers filesystem-level encryption and enables transparent encryption of files?

    A. Microsoft Encrypting File System
    B. MS-Chap
    C. BitLocker
    D. MPPE

26. What is the titled 'Guidelines for Media Sanitization' called, which is a set of standards governing data lifecycle management, especially data remanence?

    A. NIST SP 800 86
    B. NIST SP 800 83
    C. NIST SP 800 88
    D. NIST SP 800 82

27. What is a type of Man-in-the-Middle attack called that exploits Internet and security software clients' fallback to SSL 3.0, and simplifies decryption of messages?

    A. Rainbow Table
    B. Spoofing
    C. OWASP
    D. POODLE

28. What is the process of retaining different classes of important information for as long as needed, and destroying them when no longer needed, called?

    A. Record Retention

B. Material Reuse

C. Misuse Prevention

D. Fault Tolerance

29. What is the US military data classification level called that is used for restricted data which, if disclosed could cause SERIOUS damage to national security?

A. Sensitive

B. Top Secret

C. Secret

D. Confidential

30. What is the highest US military data classification level used for restricted data called, which if disclosed could cause GRAVE damage to national security?

A. Sensitive

B. Top Secret

C. Secret

D. Confidential

31. What is the data protection in storage media (USB drives) called, where the data is encrypted in the hardware through embedded encryption algorithms?

A. Full Encryption

B. Media Encryption Software

C. File Encryption Software

D. Self-encrypting USB Drive

32. Which of the following statements is true?

A. Government regulated methods for Data privacy protection in the US are PCI DSS, etc.

B. Self-regulated methods for Data privacy protection in the US are HIPAA, etc.

C. Self-regulated methods for Data privacy protection in the US are GLBA, etc.

D. Self-regulated methods for Data privacy protection in the US are PCI DSS, etc.

33. What is the part of the CFR that dictates food and drugs within the US for FDA, DEA and ONDCP?

A. Title 18

B. Title 21

C. Title 49

D. Title II

34. Which Ethernet Type, has a maximum speed of 100 Mbps, a distance of 100 meters (328 feet), has low difficulty in installation, and a low cost?

A. 10Base-T

B. 10Base5

C. 100Base-T

D. 1000Base-X

35. When a standard that helps to assign a severity score to a security vulnerability is used, what is this technique called?

A. CCSS

B. CVE

C. CCE

D. CVSS

36. Which NIST standard set of controls are used to secure Computer Systems Technology?

A. SP 500 Series

B. SP 800 Series

C. SP 260 Series

D. SP 1800 Series

37. When a system provides a reference method for publicly known computer security vulnerabilities and exposures, what is this technique called?

A. CERT

B. CVE

C. Bugtraq

D. CSIRT

38. When software tools like program editors, code analyzers, etc. are used in automated development and maintenance of software, what is this technique called?

A. Structured Development Model

B. Agile Software Development

C. CASE

D. Sashimi Software Development Model

Security Engineering

1. What is the framework designed by The Open Group for developing enterprise architecture with an understanding of a specific business environment called?

    A. ITIL

    B. SABSA

    C. TOGAF

    D. CMM

2. When a mathematical state machine model features a multilevel security policy developed by the US DoD to enforce access controls, what is this technique called?

    A. BLP

    B. Clark-Wilson

    C. Biba

    D. Chinese Wall

3. What is a mathematical state machine model featuring a multilevel computer security policy developed to enforce data integrity called?

    A. BLP

    B. Biba

    C. Chinese Wall

    D. Clark-Wilson

4. What is an integrity focused security model that prevents unauthorized and improper modifications to data, and enforces software auditing requirements called?

    A. Brewer Nash

    B. Clark Wilson

    C. Biba

    D. BLP

5. When a security model provides dynamic changes in access controls to maintain data security at times of conflicts of interest, what is this technique called?

    A. Information Flow

    B. Graham-Denning

    C. Brewer Nash

    D. Harrison-Ruzzo-Ullman

6. When a mandatory access control model defines different security levels of objects and corresponding access controls for subjects, what is this technique called?

    A. State Machine Model

    B. BLP

    C. Lattice Model

    D. Non-Interference Model

7. What is the security model that addresses the integrity of access rights of subjects by allowing them to carry out finite operations on any given object called?

    A. Brewer Nash

    B. Graham-Denning

    C. Clark Wilson

    D. Harrison-Ruzzo-Ullman

8. What is the US encryption standard for sensitive data exchange that uses the Rijndael 128-bit block symmetric cipher and 3 separate key lengths (128, 192, and 256)?

    A. IDEA

    B. AES

    C. DES

    D. 3DES

9. What is the 64-bit symmetric block cipher that performs 16 encryption rounds using a 56-bit key and was the US federal standard for sensitive unclassified data?

    A. AES

    B. DES

    C. 3DES

D. IDEA

10. What is fingerprinting a file called by secretly embedding a code into it, in order to protect the data against unauthorized use or copying?

    A. Digital Watermark

    B. Digital Signatures

    C. Digital Rights Management

    D. Digital Forensics

11. What is a symmetric key encryption algorithm that uses the DES algorithm and employs three keys to encrypt the same data in three processes, called?

    A. DES

    B. IDEA

    C. AES

    D. 3DES

12. When a system uses different keys (public-private key pairs) for encryption and decryption purposes for a higher level of security, what is this technique called?

    A. Asymmetric Cryptosystem

    B. Symmetric Cryptosystem

    C. Synchronous Cryptosystem

    D. Elliptic Curve Cryptosystem

13. When there is a complete loss of power (zero voltage) for a prolonged period, what is this concept called?

    A. Spike

    B. Sag

    C. Brownout

    D. Blackout

14. What is a 64-bit block symmetric key encryption algorithm using variable key length and putting blocks through 16 rounds of cryptographic functions, called?

    A. Blowfish

    B. CAST-128

    C. RC2

    D. AES

15. When the power supply is set at a low-voltage for a prolonged period by power companies when they experience high demand, what is this technique called?

    A. Spike

    B. Brownout

    C. Sag

    D. Blackout

16. When a list of revoked digital certificates are maintained by the certificate authority of a PKI, what is this method called?

    A. Certification Revocation List

    B. Online certificate status protocol

    C. Certificate repository

    D. Key backup and recovery system

17. When an attacker decrypts parts of a ciphertext message and then uses the decrypted data to discover the entire key, what is this attack model called?

    A. Chosen plaintext

    B. Known plaintext

    C. Chosen ciphertext

    D. Ciphertext-only

18. When an attacker encrypts parts of a plaintext message and then uses the ciphertext output to discover the entire key, what is this attack model called?

    A. Known plaintext

    B. Chosen plaintext

    C. Ciphertext-only

    D. Chosen ciphertext

19. Which of the following is a component of the Common Criteria?

    A. Identification and authentication

    B. Risk Analysis

    C. Security target

    D. Life-cycle support

20. What is a covert channel that allows relaying information to another process by modifying a resource's timing (like CPU cycles) in a predictable way, called?

    A. Side channel

    B. Covert storage channel

    C. Covert timing channel

    D. Subliminal channel

21. What is a public key algorithm that allows two parties to exchange secret keys securely through a public channel without exposing the keys, called?

    A. El Gamal

    B. Diffie Hellman

    C. Merkle-Hellman Knapsack

    D. ECC

22. What is a mathematical representation of a signature that renders nonrepudiation by verifying the signer's identity and the integrity of the document, called?

    A. Hashing

    B. Cryptography

    C. Message authentication code

    D. Digital signatures

23. What is the power degradation issue where a low-voltage condition occurs momentarily for a few seconds or for a cycle, called?

    A. Brownout

    B. Dip

    C. Blackout

    D. Spike

24. What is a special enclosure formed by a conductive material that blocks electromagnetic radiation from entering or leaving the enclosed space, called?

    A. Faraday cage

    B. White noise

    C. Control zone

    D. Anechoic chamber

25. What is the total power loss for a short period, called?

    A. Blackout

    B. Spike

    C. Fault

    D. Dip

26. What is a tool where three corners represent elements that ignite fire - fire, heat and oxygen, pointing that removal of one element would extinguish fire called?

    A. Flash point

    B. Fire triangle

    C. Fire tetrahedron

    D. Ectothermic

27. When data/message is ensured security while at rest (stored on a disk) or while in transit (transmission between parties), what is this concept called?

    A. Authentication

    B. Confidentiality

    C. Integrity

    D. Non-repudiation

28. When the data/message is ensured that it is not modified without proper authorization during its journey from sender to receiver, what is this concept called?

    A. Authentication

    B. Integrity

    C. Confidentiality

    D. Non-repudiation

29. When the claimed identity of users is verified as authentic to prevent unauthorized access, what is this concept called?

    A. Authentication

    B. Confidentiality

    C. Non-repudiation

    D. Integrity

30. When the data/message is assured that it was originated by the sender and not any unauthorized party guised as the sender, what is this concept called?

    A. Confidentiality

    B. Authentication

    C. Non-repudiation

    D. Integrity

31. When any function, using which, data of arbitrary size can be mapped to data of fixed size, what is this technique called?

    A. Digital signatures

    B. Hash Function

    C. Cryptography

    D. Message authentication code

32. What is an algorithm that converts data (mainly passwords) into a string of hash values to ensure that it is not in cleartext, providing data integrity, called?

    A. Encryption algorithm

    B. Symmetric Key algorithm

    C. Hashing algorithm

    D. Asymmetric Key algorithm

33. What is the mechanism in detection/intrusion alarm systems where the communication path between the alarm and security personnel is checked with test signals?

    A. Chemical sensor

    B. Glassbreak Detection

    C. Heartbeat sensor

    D. Motion Detector

34. When the value of an exposure to the outside environment is maintained between 40

    A. Control of Relative Humidity Value

    B. Control of Moisture

    C. Control of Relative Heating

    D. Control of Room Temperature

35. What is a patented 64-bit block cipher algorithm that uses 128 bits long key and puts the blocks through eight rounds of cryptographic functions, called?

    A. AES

    B. IDEA

    C. 3DES

    D. DES

36. When you have a level of confidence in the protection level offered by a security mechanism, what is the technique called?

    A. Assurance

    B. Testing

    C. Verification

    D. Validation

37. Which of the following is a level of TCSEC?

    A. Inadequate Assurance

    B. Labeled Security

    C. Initiating

    D. Conduct BIA

38. When a software development maturity model offers guidelines for organizations to implement meticulous software process, what is this technique called?

A. ITIL

B. TOGAF

C. SABSA

D. CMM

39. What is the full disk encryption application that is developed by Microsoft, used with a Trusted Platform Module that allows for easy management of encryptions?

A. CryptoLocker

B. EFS

C. AES

D. BitLocker

40. What is the security architecture model called where the direction of data flow amid security levels is restricted as per the guidelines in the security policy?

A. Biba Model

B. Harrison-Ruzzo-Ullman Model

C. Information flow model

D. Lattice Model

41. Which principle allows algorithms to be public and states that a cryptosystem should be secure even if everything about it, except the key, is known to all?

A. Vernam Cipher

B. Substitution Cipher

C. Kerchoff Principle

D. Scytale Cipher

42. Which of the following is a Ronald Rivest family of hashing function?

A. SHA

B. MD5

C. Tiger

D. HAVAL

43. Which of the following is an advantage of an MD5 hashing algorithm?

A. Prone to collision attacks.

B. Relatively more complex and secure than previous MD family algorithms.

C. Creates message digests of 128, 160, 192, 224, or 256 bits.

D. Operates 60

44. Which software solution manages mobile devices used by employees (company-owned or personal) to access company resources over either WiFi or mobile networks?

A. Exchange ActiveSyn (EAS)

B. Device Access Control

C. Geotagging

D. MDM

45. What is the processor mode where processes running have the highest privilege, can access system resources, and execute privileged and non-privileged instructions?

A. User mode

B. Dual-mode

C. Standalone mode

D. Kernel mode

46. What is the processor mode where processes running have limited access to resources and limited rights to execute instructions?

A. User mode

B. Kernel mode

C. Standalone mode

D. System mode

47. Which of the following statements is true?

A. Components for Common Criteria are: Protection profile
Target of evaluation
Security target

B. Components for Common Criteria are: Predictive profile
Target of evaluation
Security target

C. Components for Common Criteria are: Identification and Authentication
Target of evaluation
Security target

D. Components for Common Criteria are: Protection profile
Target of evaluation
Operational target

48. When an attacker manipulates the sequence of tasks when multiple processes are accessing the same resource to carry out tasks, what is this technique called?

A. Maintenance Hook

B. TOC/TOU

C. Race condition attack

D. Buffer Overflow

49. When an attacker uses a table of precomputed values of cryptographic hashes that contains all potential passwords for a system, what is this technique called?

A. Rainbow table attack

B. Dictionary attack

C. Social Engineering

D. Brute force attack

50. When two/more processes use the same resource at the same time, resulting in an improper order in response steps by the resource, what is this technique called?

A. Race Condition

B. Maintenance Hook

C. Race Overflow

D. TOC/TOU

51. Which of the following is a type of disaster?

A. Mitigating controls

B. Epidemics

C. Natural disasters

D. Threats

52. What is a cryptographic attack where the attacker, with the use of a plaintext message, defeats encryption algorithms that use two rounds of encryption, called?

A. Rainbow table attack

B. Meet in the middle attack

C. Man in the browser attack

D. Man in the middle attack

53. Which of the following is a power protection system?

A. Utility systems

B. Online UPS

C. HVAC systems

D. Flame detectors

54. Which cloud solution provides a holistic computing platform that includes an OS, database, and web server, and also a software solution stack?

A. SaaS

B. PaaS

C. IaaS

D. MaaS

55. What is the cloud solution that offers aspects of a data center infrastructure on demand, where companies bring and maintain their own software applications?

A. MaaS

B. IaaS

C. SaaS

D. PaaS

56. What is the cloud solution that provides users with on-demand network-based access to software applications without having to install them locally, called?

A. IaaS

B. MaaS

C. SaaS

D. PaaS

57. Which of the following is a type of cloud deployment model?

A. Community Cloud

B. Intra-Cloud

C. Macro Cloud

D. Clustering Cloud

58. When assets are available for anyone to rent and are hosted by an external cloud service provider, what is this cloud deployment model called?

A. Community Cloud

B. Public Cloud

C. Private Cloud

D. Hybrid Cloud

59. When assets are provided by the cloud service provider, but clouds are created and hosted privately by companies, what is this cloud deployment model called?

A. Community Cloud

B. Hybrid Cloud

C. Public Cloud

D. Private Cloud

60. When assets are shared by companies bound by an agreement and maintenance responsibilities are also shared, what is this cloud deployment model called?

A. Hybrid Cloud

B. Private Cloud

C. Community Cloud

D. Public Cloud

61. When there is a combination of two or more clouds, what is this cloud deployment model called?

A. Public Cloud

B. Hybrid Cloud

C. Private Cloud

D. Community Cloud

62. What is the name of the file that stores the user account information in UNIX and LINUX operating systems?

   A. /etc/passwd

   B. /etc/shadow

   C. /etc/master.passwd

   D. /etc/group

63. When a file is accessible only by the administrator and stores the encrypted passwords of user accounts in UNIX and LINUX operating systems, what is this file called?

   A. /etc/group

   B. /etc/hosts

   C. /etc/shadow

   D. /etc/passwd

64. When a combination of processes work together to ensure that specific system/database/network is always available, what is this technique called?

   A. Failover

   B. Redundancy

   C. High Availability

   D. Fault-tolerance

65. When a standard of best practices for IT processes like incident and problem management, IT financial management, etc. is adopted, what is this framework called?

   A. OCTAVE

   B. COBIT

   C. PCI-DSS

   D. ITIL

66. When a system allows diverse levels of data to be processed and makes access decisions as per the users' security clearances, what is this technique called?

   A. Discretionary Access Controls

   B. Mandatory Access Controls

   C. Multifactor authentication

   D. Multilevel Security

Security Assessment and Testing

1. What is the practice of assessing information security controls of an organization and verifying their compliance with information security standards called?

   A. Security assessment

   B. Event logging

   C. Security audit

   D. Inspection audit

2. When a chronological record of events and documentary evidence related to the user activities is maintained, what is this technique called?

   A. Audit logging

   B. User entitlement audit

   C. Event logging

   D. Account review

3. What is the open source penetration tool that automates the execution of attacks and saves testers time by removing many lengthy steps involved, called?

   A. Metasploit

   B. Snort

   C. Nessus

   D. Nmap

4. What is the method of evaluating software tests by modifying a program and analyzing the difference between the original and the mutated program versions called?

   A. Interface testing

   B. Mutation testing

   C. Misuse case testing

   D. Fuzz testing

5. When a process determines the OS used by a host of network, what is the technique called?

   A. Nmap

   B. Network Sniffing

   C. Network Scanning

   D. OS fingerprinting

6. What is the testing method that is used to verify that the change has had an expected effect after the implementation of an update/change in a software called?

A. Acceptance testing

B. Integration testing

C. Unit testing

D. Non-regression testing (NRT)

7. What is the type of scanning that sends a single packet to each scanned port with the SYN flag set, indicating a request for a new connection called?

A. TCP Connect Scanning

B. TCP SYN Scanning

C. TCP ACK Scanning

D. Ping Scanning

8. What is the type of scanning that opens a full connection to the remote system on the specified port called?

A. TCP Connect Scanning

B. TCP ACK Scanning

C. TCP SYN Scanning

D. Port Scanning

9. What is the type of scanning that sends a packet to each scanned port with the ACK flag set, indicating that it is part of an open connection called?

A. TCP SYN Scanning

B. Port Scanning

C. TCP ACK Scanning

D. TCP Connect Scanning

10. When an attacker alters normal PHP URLs and variables to remotely include and execute malicious content, what is this web vulnerability called?

A. Hard-coded credentials

B. SQL Injection

C. PHP Remote File Inclusion (RFI)

D. Cross-Site Request Forgery (CSRF)

11. When an attacker installs and runs a backdoor and exploits username/passwords left behind in the code by programmers, what is this web vulnerability called?

A. CSRF

B. PHP Remote File Inclusion (RFI)

C. Hard-coded Credentials

D. XSS

12. Which of the following is a phase of Code Review?

A. Inspection

B. Misuse Case Testing

C. Fuzzing

D. Manual Testing

Answers To Identity and Access Management

1. When user identities of two or more unrelated networks are combined without having to synchronize directory information, what is this technique called?
Answer: B

Federation

2. Which of the following statements is true?
Answer: A

IDAAS are services providing access and identity management functions to specific systems both on a company's physical premises and in the cloud.

3. Which of the following is a type of factor authentication?
Answer: A

Authentication by knowledge

4. When an access control method requires the user to use two or more factors, what is this technique called?
Answer: A

Multifactor authentication

5. When a security control tool can identify access control vulnera-bilities like unnecessary use accounts and can help mitigate them, what is this technique called?
Answer: A

Vulnerability Scanner

6. When security features are adopted to prevent unauthorized access by limiting a subject's access to an object using access rules, what is this technique called?
Answer: B

Access Control

7. What is the process of periodically checking user accounts to ensure users do not have undue privileges and deactivate dormant accounts called?
Answer: D

Account review

8. What is the process of revoking user accounts when an employee is terminated or is on an extended leave of absence to prevent fraudulent activities, called?
Answer: A

Account revocation

9. Which of the following is a Biometric authentication reference factor?
Answer: A

Signature dynamics

10. When a system accepts an unauthorized user and grants access by mistake, what is this biometric error called?
Answer: C

False Acceptance

11. When a card has the user's photograph and other identifying information that is worn as a badge and is also used to log on to systems, what is this card called?
Answer: B

CAC

12. What is the measure of the accuracy of a biometric system where the false rejection rate is equal to the false acceptance rate, called?
Answer: A

CER

13. What is the technique of asking questions about predefined responses or facts unique to a specific user that ideally cannot be answered by anyone else, called?
Answer: D

Cognitive Password

14. What is the access control type where owners of resources are allowed to define and control access to the respective resources based on their discretion called?
Answer: C

Discretionary Access Control

15. What is the ratio of Type 2 errors in biometric controls where a system accepts an unauthorized user and grants access by mistake, called?
Answer: D

FAR

16. What is the ratio of Type 1 errors in biometric controls where a system fails to verify a legitimate user and denies access, called?
Answer: A

FRR

17. What is the third party ticket authentication system based on symmetric key cryptography where the KDC shares keys with users and services for security, called?
Answer: A

Kerberos

18. Which of the following is a component of Kerberos?
Answer: C

Key Distribution Center (KDC)

19. What is a hierarchical database model for directory service information on users, clients, and processes provided by network operating systems, called?
Answer: C

LDAP

20. Tom is exploring a third-party ticket authentication system based on symmetric key where KDC shares keys with users for security. What technique is Tom using?
Answer: B

Kerberos

21. Which of the following is a step in Kerberos logon process?
Answer: B

Client encrypts username and transmits it to KDC

22. What is an access control framework where only an authoritative entity like a security administrator can decide and make changes to access levels called?
Answer: C

Non Discretionary Access Control

23. When a biometric identification method uses unique-to-each ridges, creases, and grooves on a palm verify a user's identity, what is this technique called?
Answer: D

Palm scans

24. When a user accumulates too many access rights over time without shedding any old rights, what is this technique called?
Answer: A

Privilege creep

25. What is the process of determining whether a user (new/existing) is required to have requested access as per the tasks of his role and organizational requirements called?
Answer: A

Provisioning process

26. Which of the following is a retinal scanning concern?
Answer: A

Retinal scans change during pregnancy.

27. What is an XML based convention that allows exchange of federated authentication and authorization information between security domains over web protocols called?
Answer: C

SAML

28. What is an XML-based lightweight protocol that encodes messages in a web service, decentralized, and distributed environment called?
Answer: D

SOAP

29. Which of the following is a type of Single Sign-On?
Answer: D

SESAME

30. When a KDC component is used as a trusted third party by Kerberos protocol to create tickets for user authentication, what is this technique called?
Answer: A

Ticket Granting Server

31. Which of the following is a type of Non-Discretionary Access Control?
Answer: B

Rule-based Access Control

32. Which of the following protocol is covered by the X.500 standards?
Answer: B

DISP

33. What is a non-discretionary access control model that allows users access to resources due to their organizational roles or the tasks assigned to them called?
Answer: A

RBAC

34. What is a contactless, automatic identification technology that can detect, identify and track people/objects using radio signals and electronic tags, called?
Answer: B

RFID

10

Answers To Communications and Network Security

1. When a perpetrator seeks to gain illegitimate access to a system by tampering with TCP packets and using falsified identity, what is this technique called?
Answer: B

Spoofing attack

2. What is a network application (application layer, TCP ports 20 and 21) called that allows exchange of files to and from servers which need anonymous authentication?
Answer: B

FTP

3. Which of the following best describes a weakness of FTP?
Answer: A

All data is transmitted in plaintext

4. What is the terminal emulation network application(TCP port 23) called that allows remote connectivity for command executions but doesn't allow file transfers?
Answer: D

Telnet

5. Which of the following describes a weakness of Telnet?
Answer: B

No confidentiality: all data including credentials is transmitted in plaintext.

6. What is the open-community cryptographic protocol that uses port 443, allows interoperability with other technologies and is backward compatible with SSL, called?
Answer: A

TLS

7. Which of the following describes what TLS can prevent?
Answer: A

Prevents eavesdropping and packet manipulation in VoIP.

8. Which of the following does not describe IPSec?
Answer: A

IPSec is a network protocol that was proposed as a standard by the IETF and allows data communication between network entities.

9. Which of the following is a component of IPSec?
Answer: A

Authentication Header Protocol (For integrity and authentication)

10. Which Ethernet Type, has a maximum speed of 100 Mbps, a distance of 100 meters (328 feet), has low difficulty in installation, and a low cost?
Answer: C

100Base-T

11. Which wireless security standard, is a port-based network access control which provides authentication and key management framework in wireless and wired networks?
Answer: B

802.1x

12. What is a sub-protocol of the TCP/IP protocol suite that is used to map IP network addresses to the hardware addresses used by a data link protocol called?
Answer: B

ARP

13. What is the issue caused by an attack responding to ARP broadcast queries to send falsified replies and creation of static ARP entries via ARP command called?
Answer: A

ARP cache poisoning

14. Which of the following is a common authentication protocol?
Answer: B

PAP

15. When a hacker gains unauthorized connection through Bluetooth devices to access contact lists, emails, etc. on the target system, what is this technique called?
Answer: A

Bluesnarfing attack

16. Which of the following is a type of Bluetooth-based attack?
Answer: C

Bluesnarfing attack

17. Amy is examining attacks that use Cain and Abel password cracking programs having rainbow tables to recover passwords on Windows. What technique is Amy seeking?
Answer: B

CAIN attack

18. What is a group of networked systems that compete for the same communication medium and cause a collision if two or more systems transmit at the same time called?
Answer: B

Collision domain

19. What is a LAN media access technology used in Ethernet networks reacting to collisions and making collision domain members wait before starting processes called?
Answer: D

CSMA/CD

20. When an attacker beats the real replies from a valid DNS server by sending false replies to a requesting system, what is this technique called?
Answer: B

DNS Spoofing

21. When an attacker redirects traffic to a malicious system or performs a DoS attack by changing domain-name-to-IP-address mappings, what is this technique called?

Answer: C

DNS Poisoning

22. Which of the following is a security issue for Faxes?

Answer: B

Faxed data is printed automatically and accessible easily by all.

23. Which of the following is NOT a security issue for Faxes?

Answer: B

Faxed data transmitted through Fax servers can be logged and audited.

24. When traffic is filtered based on the application used to exchange data and the origin of the data using proxy servers are masked, what is this technique called?

Answer: A

Firewall - second generation

25. What is a WAN protocol running at data link layer and using packet-switching technology to allow network interfaces to share the same WAN connection called?

Answer: D

Frame relay

26. Which layer in the OSI model converts bits into electrical signals, and controls electrical, optical and mechanical requirements of data transmission?

Answer: B

Physical Layer

27. Which layer in the OSI model converts data into LAN or WAN frames to allow transmission, defining how a system will access a network?

Answer: B

Data-Link Layer

28. Which layer in the OSI model is concerned with internetworking service, addressing, and routing?

Answer: A

Network Layer

29. Which layer in the OSI model sets up connections between applications, maintains dialog control and negotiates, maintains and takes down communication channels?

Answer: A

Session Layer

30. Which layer in the OSI model is concerned with compression and decompression of data, encryption and decryption of data, and translations into standard formats?

Answer: C

Presentation Layer

31. Which layer in the OSI model is concerned with file transfer, fulfilling networking requests of applications, network management, and virtual terminals?

Answer: B

Application Layer

32. What is a network layer protocol that delivers status and error messages, reports routing information, and helps test connectivity on IP networks, called?

Answer: D

ICMP

33. Which of the following is a common Instant Messaging protocol?
Answer: A

IRC

34. What is an IP-based SAN protocol that allows linking of data storage facilities, location-independent data storage, transmission and retrieval on Internet called?
Answer: A

iSCSI

35. When a technology breaks telephone lines into channels and allows them to transmit data, voice, and other source traffic digitally, what is this technique called?
Answer: D

ISDN

36. Which of the following does not describe LEAP?
Answer: B

LEAP is more secure due to encryption.

37. Which of the following does not describe PEAP?
Answer: C

PEAP is Password based.

38. Which of the following best describes a task group of the 802.11 standards?
Answer: D

802.11e: QoS

39. Which of the following best describes a frequency of a task group of the 802.11 standards?
Answer: A

802.11b: 2.4 GHz

40. Which TCP port is used by Microsoft SQL Server?
Answer: C

Port 1443

41. What is an IP address(usually 127.0.0.1) used in machine level self-diagnosis and troubleshooting by creating an interface to connect to itself via TCP/IP called?
Answer: B

Loopback address

42. When a factory assigned MAC address of a network interface is changed on a networked device, what is this technique called?
Answer: C

MAC spoofing

43. What is a high-throughput networking technology that directs data across a network based on short path labels instead of long network addresses called?
Answer: B

MPLS

44. What is the process of controlling traffic among networked devices by splitting the network into individual network segments, called?
Answer: D

Network segmentation

45. Which of the following is a type of Network topology?
Answer: C

Star

46. Which of the following is a layer in the OSI model?
Answer: D

Presentation

47. Which of the following is a security issue for a PBX?
Answer: D

Phreakers can hack and alter voice messages leading to brute force and other attacks.

48. What is an attack where a telephone system is hacked using various types of technology and used to make free and/or long-distance calls, steal services, called?
Answer: D

Phreaking

49. Which of the following is a tool employed for Phreaking?
Answer: C

Black boxes

50. Which protocol provides a graphical interface which enables a computer to connect to another computer over a network connection?
Answer: D

RDP

51. Which networking device is used to amplify data signals by repeating them between cable segments to physically extend the range of a network?
Answer: D

Repeater

52. Which networking device connects similar/different networks by opening data packets, reading network addresses and sending to the right networks?
Answer: B

Router

53. What is a distance vector routing protocol that defines the exchanging of routing table data through routers using hop count as a metric called?
Answer: A

RIP

54. Which of the following statements is true?
Answer: A

802.1x is a wireless security standard that is a port-based network access control which provides authentication and key management framework in wireless and wired networks.

55. Which of the following statements is true?
Answer: D

Type of Bluetooth-based attacks are: Bluejacking Bluebugging Bluesnarfing

56. When two/more systems collide by transmitting data at the same time to a connection that only supports a single transmission path, what is the technique called?
Answer: B

Collision

57. Port 21 is employed by which service?
Answer: C

FTP

58. Port 25 is used by which service?
Answer: D

SMTP

59. Which service employs Port 80?
Answer: A

HTTP

60. Port 123 is employed by which service?
Answer: B

NTP

61. Which service employs Port 161/162?
Answer: C

SNMP

62. 135/UDP server port is employed by which service?
Answer: A

NetBIOS

63. When a networking protocol synchronizes clocks of network components with a central clock source to ensure operational stability, what is this protocol called?
Answer: A

NTP

64. Which of the following is an IP address range outlined in RFC 1918?
Answer: C

10.0.0.0-10.255.255.255 - Class A network

65. What is the wireless access protocol that provides 64-bit, 128-bit and 256-bit encryption using the Rivest Ciper4 (RC4) algorithm to protect wireless data called?
Answer: D

WEP

66. What is the wireless access protocol that addresses the weaknesses of WEP by implementing TKIP, called?
Answer: C

WPA

67. What is the wireless access protocol that provides more secure algorithms by including AES cryptography?
Answer: C

WPA2

68. What is the network discovery scanning technique that sends a packet with all TCP flags (FIN, PSH and URG) set, or lit up like a Christmas tree?
Answer: C

Xmas scan

69. When a VoIP Quality of Service issue occurs due to variation in latency in various packets affecting the quality of conversations, what is the technique called?
Answer: D

Jitter

70. Which is the VoIP Quality of Service factor that refers to the time it takes for a packet to travel from a host server to the destination?
Answer: C

Latency

71. What is the cryptographic attack where an attacker maliciously intercepts communication and controls, alters or eliminates the data being exchanged, called?
Answer: C

Man in the middle attack

72. When one or more packets of data are lost between source and destination due to network congestion, what is this technique called?
Answer: D

Packet Loss

73. What is an approach to virtualizing network operation, design, and management, allowing for routing decisions to be made remotely, called?
Answer: C

SDN

74. When a target network is flooded with a series of SYN packets and then ignored by the spoofed source causing it to crash, what is this technique called?

Answer: D

SYN Flood Attack

75. When a target system is flooded with numerous spoofed ping requests, leaving it with no time to respond to legitimate requests, what is this technique called?

Answer: C

Ping Flood Attack

76. When spoofed broadcast/echo ICMP packets are sent to a target system's network broadcast address drawing traffic on the network, what is the technique called?

Answer: D

Smurf Attack

77. When UDP packets with spoofed IP address of a victim are sent to a target system's network broadcast address attracting traffic, what is this technique called?

Answer: D

Fraggle Attack

78. When a network device limits access from one network to another, internally and externally, and filters malicious internet traffic, what is this technique called?

Answer: A

Firewall

79. Which of the following filtering rule can be used to prevent IP spoofing?

Answer: B

Packets with internal source IP addresses don't enter the network.

80. When a hybrid vulnerability scanning tool is used to scan both the network and the web for vulnerabilities, what is this tool called?

Answer: D

Nessus

81. When a network discovery scanning tool is used to check the state of network ports and discover hosts and services to create a map of it, what is this tool called?

Answer: A

Nmap

11

Answers To Software Development Security

1. What are shortcuts installed by programmers called to bypass system checks during development that become security threats if not removed before the release?
   Answer: A

   Maintenance hook

2. When an attacker with limited access manages to gain access to additional resources beyond his access rights, what is this technique called?
   Answer: D

   Privilege escalation

3. Which of the following can be classified as a Programming Language generation?
   Answer: A

   Natural Language

4. Which of the following is NOT a type of Programming Language Generations?
   Answer: D

   Expert Language

5. Which of the following is a type of ACID integrity components?
   Answer: A

   Atomicity

6. When pieces of less sensitive information are combined to provide new information of a higher sensitivity level beyond the user's access rights, what is this concept called?
   Answer: D

   Aggregating functions

7. When software is developed using an interactive and incremental development model that encourages flexibility, adaptability and team collaboration, what is this process called?
   Answer: D

   Agile

8. Which of the following is a type of Artificial Intelligence systems?
   Answer: A

   Expert Systems

9. When an interaction between a web application and another application/OS/database is allowed, what is the technique called and what is the code that acts as pass-

words on function calls called?

Answer: D

API and API Keys

10. When a network of several systems stands compromised with zombie codes, and is used to send spam/phishing emails, what is the technique called?

Answer: C

Botnet

11. When a variable is checked if it is within specified limits or constraints before it is used, what is this method called?

Answer: C

Bounds Checking

12. When an attacker seeks to flood a system with more data than the buffer allows and thus causing system failure or compromise, what is this method called?

Answer: C

Buffer Overflow

13. When software tools like program editors, code analyzers, etc. are used in automated development and maintenance of software, what is this technique called?

Answer: C

CASE

14. When the changes that occur during any phase of a system life cycle are controlled and the change control activities are documented, what is this process called?

Answer: D

Change Control

15. Which of the following is a stage in the Change Control process?

Answer: B

Change request

16. While developing a product when the focus is on defect prevention that is achieved by structured methods during developing and testing, what is this model called?

Answer: D

Cleanroom

17. When the ability of a program to perform different types of tasks independently without interacting with any other programs is measured, what is this technique called?

Answer: B

Cohesion

18. When a perpetrator attacks through unauthorized commands that are executed in an OS through a vulnerable application, what is this technique called?

Answer: C

Command Injection

19. When a program converts high-level source code into an executable binary file targeted for a specific OS, what is this language called?

Answer: A

Compiled Language

20. When a program executes instructions without previously compiling into machine language, but is prone to malicious code insertion, what is this language called?

Answer: A

Interpreted Language

21. When a process ensures that the changes made to software versions are in line with the change control and configuration management requirements, what is

this technique called?
Answer: B

Configuration Control

22. Which of the following is a stage in the Configuration Management process?
Answer: C

Configuration Status Accounting

23. When the level of interaction a module needs to make with other programs to carry out its tasks is measured, what is this technique called?
Answer: B

Coupling

24. When a web attack uses 3rd party redirect of static connect within the security context of a trusted site, what is this technique called?
Answer: D

CSRF

25. When a database for system developers records all data structures used by a particular application including sources, type, etc., what is this technique called?
Answer: B

Data Dictionary

26. When multiple users or applications try to extract data concurrently and some preventive controls maintain the integrity of data, what is this technique called?
Answer: B

Database Concurrency

27. When discrete sets of SQL instructions are used by relational databases to ensure data security, what is this technique called?
Answer: A

Database transactions

28. When a development approach is adopted focusing on three elements- software development, quality assurance and IT operations, what is this approach called?
Answer: C

DevOps

29. When an attacker seeks to traverse inaccessible directories by inserting the characters "../" many times into the URL, what is this technique called?
Answer: C

Directory traversal attack

30. When vulnerabilities of a software is publicly disclosed by its researchers without any restrictions, what is this approach called?
Answer: C

Full Disclosure

31. Which of the following is a way to protect against a SQL Injection attack?
Answer: D

Limiting account privileges

32. Which of the following is a phase of the IDEAL software development model?
Answer: C

Acting

33. When a user deduces information that is not explicitly available, what is this technique called?
Answer: A

Inference

34. When a user has access to particular information and is able to deduce information that she is not authorized to access, what is

this attack called?

Answer: C

Inference attack

35. When security characteristics of the main class (super/parent class) are inherited automatically by subclasses, what is this technique called?

Answer: D

Inheritance

36. When a platform independent virus, written in Word Basic, Visual Basic or VBScript macro languages, infects documents and templates, what is this virus called?

Answer: D

Macro virus

37. Which of the following is a type of a Malware?

Answer: B

Logic Bombs

38. Which of the following is a Malware detection technique?

Answer: C

Known Signature Scanning

39. When bootable media portions (single disk sectors) are used by a computer to load an operating system during the boot process, what is this technique called?

Answer: A

Master boot record

40. When a virus attacks the MBR by redirecting system to infected boot sector loading the virus before the OS during the boot process, what is this virus called?

Answer: C

MBR Virus

41. When a programming language model is organized around self-sufficient reusable objects that combine methods and data, what is this model called?

Answer: C

OOP

42. When the source code of a software program is made available to anyone, what is this approach called?

Answer: A

Open Source

43. What is OWASP?

Answer: B

OWASP is an open nonprofit project which helps improve the security of web-based application software and free sharing of methodologies and techniques in the area.

44. When security vulnerabilities of a software/hardware are disclosed to the vendor, giving a chance to fix flaws and release a patch, what is this approach called?

Answer: C

Partial Disclosure

45. When a preventive measure against password-cracking is adopted along with a set of rules for users to create strong passwords, what is this technique called?

Answer: D

Password policy

12

Answers To Security and Risk Management

1. What is the value that denotes the predicted frequency of a particular risk which is realized within a year called?
Answer: B

   ARO

2. Which of the following is a phase of the BCP?
Answer: D

   Continuity Planning

3. Which of the following is stage in the BCP?
Answer: C

   BCP training

4. Which law mandates all communications service providers to make wiretap option available for law enforcement agencies irrespective of the technology used?
Answer: B

   CALEA

5. When an alternate control providing the same level of security as the original one is chosen due to cost/business requirements, what is this technique called?
Answer: C

   Compensating Control

6. Which law regulates the collection of information from children by websites, and mandates sites to provide privacy notice and operator contact details?
Answer: C

   COPPA Act

7. When an assignable legal right protects an author's work from unauthorized duplication, what is this technique called?
Answer: C

   Copyright

8. When a perpetrator prevents authorized users from accessing resources by malicious traffic flooding or exploiting design flaws, what is this technique called?
Answer: C

   Denial of service (DoS)

9. When post facto access controls are deployed to detect the activities of an unauthorized incident and to identify intruders, what is

this technique called?
Answer: C

Detective controls

10. Luke wants to adopt access control measures that discourage intruders from attacking or warm them not to attack. What technique should Luke use?
Answer: B

Deterrent Controls

11. When an entity uses reasonable care, prudent management, and common sense to protect its interests, what is this technique called?
Answer: D

Due Care

12. Which law penalizes the theft of trade secrets from U.S. corporations or government agencies with or without intending to benefit a foreign government?
Answer: A

Economic Espionage Act

13. Which law protects individuals against unlawful monitoring or disclosure of electronic communication including voicemails, emails, and mobile phone calls?
Answer: B

ECPA

14. Which US law allows financial institutions like banks and insurance companies to provide a variety of services and share customer information among themselves?
Answer: B

Gramm Leach Bliley Act

15. When an unauthorized user takes advantage of a system design vulnerability to access private, confidential or controlled information, what is the attack called?
Answer: C

Information disclosure

16. What is the security standard that defines the requirements for the establishment, control, and implementation of an information security management system?
Answer: A

ISO 27001

17. When a security standard outlines the code of practice for information security management, what is this standard called?
Answer: A

ISO 27002

18. What is the technique that defines the maximum period of downtime that can be endured by a business function before any irreversible damage is caused?
Answer: D

MTO

19. Which of the following is a stage of the NIST SP800-34?
Answer: C

Performing Business Impact Analysis

20. When access control mechanisms are stationed to protect systems, personnel, and other resources within a facility, what is this technique called?
Answer: A

Physical Controls

21. When proactive control systems are adopted to keep unauthorized

activities from occurring in the first place, what is this technique called?

Answer: D

Preventive controls

22. When a part of the federal sentencing guidelines calls for executives to take ownership of processes as prudent persons would do, what is this approach called?

Answer: C

Prudent man rule

23. When a subjective method of assessing risk is used by ranking threat scenarios instead of calculating monetary figures of losses, what is this technique called?

Answer: C

Qualitative Risk Assessment

24. Which of the following is a step of Quantitative risk analysis?

Answer: A

Calculate ARO

25. When countermeasures are implemented to reduce risk levels, to block threats and remove weaknesses, what is this process called?

Answer: D

Risk Mitigation

26. When risks and any costs of losses are shifted from one party to another, what is this strategy called?

Answer: C

Risk Transference

27. What is the metric used in disaster recovery that defines the acceptable amount of data loss, measured in time?

Answer: A

RPO

28. When a perpetrator gains illegitimate access to a system by tampering with the TCP packets and using falsified identity, what is this technique called?

Answer: C

Spoofing

29. Which of the following is not a step of the Business Impact Analysis?

Answer: A

Make a formal request for change.

30. When a perpetrator attacks to alter, falsify or manipulate data without authorization while in storage or transit, what is this technique called?

Answer: C

Tampering

31. What is the critical intellectual property of a company which, if made public could harm the company's profitability and survival?

Answer: B

Trade Secret

32. What is the technique that protects certain words, symbols, slogans, and logos that represent a company, its brands, and its products or services called?

Answer: C

Trademark

33. What is the security tool that is used to identify weaknesses against potential threats in the systems as well as control mechanisms of an organization?

Answer: A

Vulnerability Assessment

34. Who is the person that is responsible for creating the information security program and appropriately funding, staffing and has organizational priority?

Answer: B

Business Owner

35. What is the regulation passed by the European Parliament intending to strengthen protection of personal data for individuals within the European Union, called?

Answer: A

EU GDPR

36. Which US law binds all federal agencies, government contractors, and vendors to have information security programs to protect federal information systems?

Answer: D

FISMA

37. What is the preventive access control method which can prevent fraud by making it impossible for only one individual to access sensitive resources?

Answer: D

Separation Of Duties

38. What is the framework of IT security best practices that recommend security control requirements, ensuring IT security is aligned with company's goals called?

Answer: D

COBIT

39. Which of the following best describes the ISC2 code of ethics?

Answer: D

Protect society, the commonwealth, and the infrastructure.

40. When a security principle allows authorized users timely and uninterrupted access to resources, what is this technique called?

Answer: A

Availability

41. What is the security principle that ensures secrecy of objects, data, and resources and protects them against unauthorized disclosure, called?

Answer: A

Confidentiality

42. What is the security principle that assures the accuracy of resources by eliminating risks of unauthorized modification, called?

Answer: C

Integrity

43. When an attacker tricks users into disclosing sensitive information through emails or links to websites that look legitimate, what is this technique called?

Answer: B

Phishing

44. Which of the following is a stage in penetration testing methodology?

Answer: A

Reconnaissance

45. What is a threat modeling tool that graphically represents all the ways in which specific threats can be realized, called?

Answer: B

Threat tree

13

Answers To Security Operations

1. What is an alternate processing site equipped for emergencies with basic environmental and electrical support, but no computing facilities called?
Answer: A

Cold site

2. What is an alternate processing site having basic infrastructure and a few extra facilities like HVAC, but not any communication or computing systems, called?
Answer: B

Warm Site

3. What is a fully configured backup facility equipped with communications links, server, and workstations that can be operational in just a few hours called?
Answer: C

Hot Site

4. When a reciprocal agreement binds two organizations to help each other in case of emergency situations, what is this technique called?
Answer: D

Mutual aid agreement

5. What is a suite of technologies that can detect and block data exfiltration attempts by scanning keywords preventing loss of sensitive information, called?
Answer: B

DLP system

6. What is a high volume electronic mailing list that discusses computer security issues covering vulnerabilities, methods of exploitation, solutions, etc. called?
Answer: B

Bugtraq

7. What is a suite of security solutions that detect and block data exfiltration attempts by scanning data, looking for data patterns and keywords, called?
Answer: D

DLP

8. Which of the following is a step in the Disaster recovery process?
Answer: B

Assess Damage

9. Which of the following best describes a type of trusted recovery?
Answer: A

Trusted recovery performed
manually by an administrator after a crash.

10. Which of the following is a physical control?
Answer: C

Mantrap

11. What is a physical control in the
form of an entry gate called that
prevents tailgating by allowing
only one person in one direction
per authentication?
Answer: C

Turnstile

12. What is an intrusion detection
control that senses and uses
movement to identify presence in
a controlled area, called?
Answer: D

Motion detector

13. What is the control mechanism
that triggers a notification to alert
responders in case of an intrusion
called?
Answer: C

Alarm system

14. What is a visual recording device called that transmits videos
to screens monitored by the security personnel to the detect presence of intruders?
Answer: D

CCTV camera

15. Which motion detector is designed to detect meaningful
changes in the infrared lighting
pattern of a given area?
Answer: C

Infrared motion detector

16. Which of the following is a RAID
level?
Answer: D

Interleave parity

17. What is the team responsible
for identifying, monitoring, and
responding to computer security incidents in an organization,
called?
Answer: A

CSIRT

18. What is the unused portion of a
network's allocated IP addresses,
called?
Answer: C

Darknet

19. What is the type of database
backup where the remote server
is updated with copies of
database modifications in real-
time as they are to the production server?
Answer: B

Remote Mirroring

20. What is the type of database
recovery where actual files are
copied as they are modified and
periodically transferred to an offsite facility called?
Answer: A

Electronic Vaulting

21. What is a method of data backup
where data is backed up on tapes
and transferred either manually
or electronically to an offsite facility called?
Answer: A

Tape Vaulting

22. When a replication happens
in real-time across repositories,

what is this technique called?

Answer: A

Synchronous Replication

23. When a system continues to operate despite suffering a single component fault, what is this technique called?

Answer: C

Fault Tolerance

24. What is a type of intrusion detection system that is installed on a host computer to monitor anomalous activity and report it to the administrator, called?

Answer: C

HIDS

25. What is a pseudo flawed system set-up like a genuine system on a network with valid resources to lure intruders and keep them away from the live network called?

Answer: C

Honeypot systems

26. What is the process of detecting an issue, finding its cause, minimizing the damage, resolving the issue, and documenting these response steps, called?

Answer: D

Incident Response

27. Which of the following is a step in the Incident response process?

Answer: B

Remediation

28. When a document records the intention of two parties to work together to achieve a common goal, what is this method called?

Answer: D

MOU

29. When an administrative control principle allows users access only to resources that they need to perform their jobs, what is this method called?

Answer: C

Need to Know

30. What is an agreement between two departments of an organization describing the level of service expected, service measurement metrics, penalties, etc. called?

Answer: B

OLA

31. Which of the following is a requirement for any evidence to be admissible in court?

Answer: D

Properly Identified

32. When administrators assign rights to users depending on the type of privileged operation instead of granting unrestricted access, what is this technique called?

Answer: D

Separation of privileges

33. What are a suite of updates, enhancements or fixes to a software delivered to the user as a single installable package, called?

Answer: C

Service Pack

34. What is a project management document that describes the product and customer requirements and defines deliverables, project-specific activities and timelines called?

Answer: B

SOW

35. Which of the following statements is true?

Answer: C

Database recovery and its types are: Remote Mirroring Remote Journaling Electronic Vaulting

36. Which of the following statements is true?

Answer: C

Synchronous Replication is a replication that happens in real-time across repositories.

37. When a system recovers after failure in an open state providing all access, what is this technique called?

Answer: B

Fail-open state

38. When a primary system fails or goes offline and a critical fault-tolerant function makes a standby system available automatically, what is this technique called?

Answer: C

Failover

39. When a system not only detects but is also equipped to block attacks to a target system before they occur, what is this technique called?

Answer: D

Intrusion prevention systems

14

Answers To Asset Security

1. When regulations by US DoC are adopted to prevent unauthorized cross-border data disclosure, what is this policy called?
Answer: A

EU safe harbor privacy principles

2. Which of the following is a standard metric for the Application Security business function of the CIS Security Benchmark?
Answer: A

Risk assessment coverage

3. Which of the following is a standard metric for the Configuration Change Management business function of the CIS Security Benchmark?
Answer: B

Mean-time to complete changes

4. Which of the following is a standard metric for the Financial Management business function of the CIS Security Benchmark?
Answer: C

InfoSec budget as percentage of IT budget

5. Which of the following is a standard metric for the Incident Management business function of the CIS Security Benchmark?
Answer: D

Detection by internal controls (

6. Which of the following is a standard metric for the Patch Management business function of the CIS Security Benchmark?
Answer: B

Mean-time to patch

7. Which of the following is a standard metric for the Vulnerability Management business function of the CIS Security Benchmark?
Answer: D

Vulnerability scan coverage

8. Who is the person responsible for creating and assigning rights to user accounts as per classification rules and access control policies?
Answer: D

Classification Administrator

9. Who is the person responsible for the actual system that houses and/or processes sensitive data

and is responsible for the security of the data during processing?
Answer: D

Classification System Owner

10. Who is the person who routinely accesses data through a computing system for work-related tasks?
Answer: D

Classification User

11. What is the label for the data ordered above the unclassified level in the US military data classification and exempt from laws like the Freedom of Information Act?
Answer: D

Classified

12. What is the label for the highest level of classification of data in commercial businesses which means the data is most sensitive and for internal use only?
Answer: C

Confidential

13. When the protection of data is achieved through whole-disk, database, PGP, or other kinds of software-based encryption programs, what is this technique called?
Answer: B

Data at rest protection

14. What is the data classification label where the data should stay internal to the business and any infringement could cause grave damage to the organization?
Answer: D

Private

15. When data protection is achieved through transport encryption

protocols like IPSec, SSL, and SSH, what is this technique called?
Answer: B

Data in Transit

16. When data is placed in temporary storage buffers while being used by an application, what is this technique called?
Answer: B

Data in Use

17. What is the data classification process called, where labels are assigned to electronic data, or physically marked in the case of data objects?
Answer: B

Data labeling

18. Which of the following is a government regulated method for Data privacy protection in the US?
Answer: B

GLBA

19. Who is the person or entity, usually a third party vendor, that processes personal data on behalf of a data controller?
Answer: D

Data processor

20. What is the residual magnetic flux called that remains on the hard drive as a physical representation of the data after erasure?
Answer: D

Data remanence

21. What is the destruction of data from a system using a trusted method, which could be a combination of processes, to make sure

it cannot be recovered, called?
Answer: B

Data sanitization

22. What is the process of removing or reducing the security classification on a media or a system called, in order to reuse it in an unclassified environment?
Answer: C

Declassification

23. Which of the following is a EU Data Protection principle?
Answer: C

Shall be dealt with appropriate measures to protect against accidental loss or damage.

24. What is the technology called that provides superior security that partial encryption like encryption of files/folders by encrypting the data on the disk?
Answer: D

Full disk encryption

25. What is a cryptographic feature on Microsoft Windows called that offers filesystem-level encryption and enables transparent encryption of files?
Answer: A

Microsoft Encrypting File System

26. What is the titled 'Guidelines for Media Sanitization' called, which is a set of standards governing data lifecycle management, especially data remanence?
Answer: C

NIST SP 800 88

27. What is a type of Man-in-the-Middle attack called that exploits Internet and security software clients' fallback to SSL 3.0, and simplifies decryption of messages?
Answer: D

POODLE

28. What is the process of retaining different classes of important information for as long as needed, and destroying them when no longer needed, called?
Answer: A

Record Retention

29. What is the US military data classification level called that is used for restricted data which, if disclosed could cause SERIOUS damage to national security?
Answer: C

Secret

30. What is the highest US military data classification level used for restricted data called, which if disclosed could cause GRAVE damage to national security?
Answer: B

Top Secret

31. What is the data protection in storage media (USB drives) called, where the data is encrypted in the hardware through embedded encryption algorithms?
Answer: D

Self-encrypting USB Drive

32. Which of the following statements is true?
Answer: D

Self-regulated methods for Data privacy protection in the US are PCI DSS, etc.

33. What is the part of the CFR that dictates food and drugs

within the US for FDA, DEA and ONDCP?

Answer: B

Title 21

34. Which Ethernet Type, has a maximum speed of 100 Mbps, a distance of 100 meters (328 feet), has low difficulty in installation, and a low cost?

Answer: C

100Base-T

35. When a standard that helps to assign a severity score to a security vulnerability is used, what is this technique called?

Answer: D

CVSS

36. Which NIST standard set of controls are used to secure Computer Systems Technology?

Answer: A

SP 500 Series

37. When a system provides a reference method for publicly known computer security vulnerabilities and exposures, what is this technique called?

Answer: B

CVE

38. When software tools like program editors, code analyzers, etc. are used in automated development and maintenance of software, what is this technique called?

Answer: C

CASE

15

Answers To Security Engineering

1. What is the framework designed by The Open Group for developing enterprise architecture with an understanding of a specific business environment called?
Answer: C
TOGAF

2. When a mathematical state machine model features a multilevel security policy developed by the US DoD to enforce access controls, what is this technique called?
Answer: A
BLP

3. What is a mathematical state machine model featuring a multilevel computer security policy developed to enforce data integrity called?
Answer: B
Biba

4. What is an integrity focused security model that prevents unauthorized and improper modifications to data, and enforces software auditing requirements called?
Answer: B

Clark Wilson

5. When a security model provides dynamic changes in access controls to maintain data security at times of conflicts of interest, what is this technique called?
Answer: C
Brewer Nash

6. When a mandatory access control model defines different security levels of objects and corresponding access controls for subjects, what is this technique called?
Answer: C
Lattice Model

7. What is the security model that addresses the integrity of access rights of subjects by allowing them to carry out finite operations on any given object called?
Answer: D
Harrison-Ruzzo-Ullman

8. What is the US encryption standard for sensitive data exchange that uses the Rijndael 128-bit block symmetric cipher and 3 separate key lengths (128, 192,

and 256)?
Answer: B

AES

9. What is the 64-bit symmetric block cipher that performs 16 encryption rounds using a 56-bit key and was the US federal standard for sensitive unclassified data?
Answer: B

DES

10. What is fingerprinting a file called by secretly embedding a code into it, in order to protect the data against unauthorized use or copying?
Answer: A

Digital Watermark

11. What is a symmetric key encryption algorithm that uses the DES algorithm and employs three keys to encrypt the same data in three processes, called?
Answer: D

3DES

12. When a system uses different keys (public-private key pairs) for encryption and decryption purposes for a higher level of security, what is this technique called?
Answer: A

Asymmetric Cryptosystem

13. When there is a complete loss of power (zero voltage) for a prolonged period, what is this concept called?
Answer: D

Blackout

14. What is a 64-bit block symmetric key encryption algorithm using variable key length and putting blocks through 16 rounds of cryptographic functions, called?
Answer: A

Blowfish

15. When the power supply is set at a low-voltage for a prolonged period by power companies when they experience high demand, what is this technique called?
Answer: B

Brownout

16. When a list of revoked digital certificates are maintained by the certificate authority of a PKI, what is this method called?
Answer: A

Certification Revocation List

17. When an attacker decrypts parts of a ciphertext message and then uses the decrypted data to discover the entire key, what is this attack model called?
Answer: C

Chosen ciphertext

18. When an attacker encrypts parts of a plaintext message and then uses the ciphertext output to discover the entire key, what is this attack model called?
Answer: B

Chosen plaintext

19. Which of the following is a component of the Common Criteria?
Answer: C

Security target

20. What is a covert channel that allows relaying information to another process by modifying a resource's timing (like CPU cycles)

in a predictable way, called?
Answer: C

Covert timing channel

21. What is a public key algorithm that allows two parties to exchange secret keys securely through a public channel without exposing the keys, called?
Answer: B

Diffie Hellman

22. What is a mathematical representation of a signature that renders nonrepudiation by verifying the signer's identity and the integrity of the document, called?
Answer: D

Digital signatures

23. What is the power degradation issue where a low-voltage condition occurs momentarily for a few seconds or for a cycle, called?
Answer: B

Dip

24. What is a special enclosure formed by a conductive material that blocks electromagnetic radiation from entering or leaving the enclosed space, called?
Answer: A

Faraday cage

25. What is the total power loss for a short period, called?
Answer: C

Fault

26. What is a tool where three corners represent elements that ignite fire - fire, heat and oxygen, pointing that removal of one element would extinguish fire called?
Answer: B

Fire triangle

27. When data/message is ensured security while at rest (stored on a disk) or while in transit (transmission between parties), what is this concept called?
Answer: B

Confidentiality

28. When the data/message is ensured that it is not modified without proper authorization during its journey from sender to receiver, what is this concept called?
Answer: B

Integrity

29. When the claimed identity of users is verified as authentic to prevent unauthorized access, what is this concept called?
Answer: A

Authentication

30. When the data/message is assured that it was originated by the sender and not any unauthorized party guised as the sender, what is this concept called?
Answer: C

Non-repudiation

31. When any function, using which, data of arbitrary size can be mapped to data of fixed size, what is this technique called?
Answer: B

Hash Function

32. What is an algorithm that converts data (mainly passwords) into a string of hash values to ensure that it is not in cleartext, providing data integrity, called?
Answer: C

Hashing algorithm

33. What is the mechanism in detection/intrusion alarm systems where the communication path between the alarm and security personnel is checked with test signals?
Answer: C

Heartbeat sensor

34. When the value of an exposure to the outside environment is maintained between 40

Control of Relative Humidity Value

35. What is a patented 64-bit block cipher algorithm that uses 128 bits long key and puts the blocks through eight rounds of cryptographic functions, called?
Answer: B

IDEA

36. When you have a level of confidence in the protection level offered by a security mechanism, what is the technique called?
Answer: A

Assurance

37. Which of the following is a level of TCSEC?
Answer: B

Labeled Security

38. When a software development maturity model offers guidelines for organizations to implement meticulous software process, what is this technique called?
Answer: D

CMM

39. What is the full disk encryption application that is developed by Microsoft, used with a Trusted Platform Module that allows for easy management of encryptions?
Answer: D

BitLocker

40. What is the security architecture model called where the direction of data flow amid security levels is restricted as per the guidelines in the security policy?
Answer: C

Information flow model

41. Which principle allows algorithms to be public and states that a cryptosystem should be secure even if everything about it, except the key, is known to all?
Answer: C

Kerchoff Principle

42. Which of the following is a Ronald Rivest family of hashing function?
Answer: B

MD5

43. Which of the following is an advantage of an MD5 hashing algorithm?
Answer: B

Relatively more complex and secure than previous MD family algorithms.

44. Which software solution manages mobile devices used by employees (company-owned or personal) to access company resources over either WiFi or mobile networks?
Answer: D

MDM

45. What is the processor mode where processes running have the

highest privilege, can access system resources, and execute privileged and non-privileged instructions?
Answer: D

Kernel mode

46. What is the processor mode where processes running have limited access to resources and limited rights to execute instructions?
Answer: A

User mode

47. Which of the following statements is true?
Answer: A

Components for Common Criteria are: Protection profile

Target of evaluation

Security target

48. When an attacker manipulates the sequence of tasks when multiple processes are accessing the same resource to carry out tasks, what is this technique called?
Answer: C

Race condition attack

49. When an attacker uses a table of precomputed values of cryptographic hashes that contains all potential passwords for a system, what is this technique called?
Answer: A

Rainbow table attack

50. When two/more processes use the same resource at the same time, resulting in an improper order in response steps by the resource, what is this technique called?
Answer: A

Race Condition

51. Which of the following is a type of disaster?
Answer: C

Natural disasters

52. What is a cryptographic attack where the attacker, with the use of a plaintext message, defeats encryption algorithms that use two rounds of encryption, called?
Answer: B

Meet in the middle attack

53. Which of the following is a power protection system?
Answer: B

Online UPS

54. Which cloud solution provides a holistic computing platform that includes an OS, database, and web server, and also a software solution stack?
Answer: B

PaaS

55. What is the cloud solution that offers aspects of a data center infrastructure on demand, where companies bring and maintain their own software applications?
Answer: B

IaaS

56. What is the cloud solution that provides users with on-demand network-based access to software applications without having to install them locally, called?
Answer: C

SaaS

57. Which of the following is a type of cloud deployment model?
Answer: A

Community Cloud

58. When assets are available for anyone to rent and are hosted by an external cloud service provider, what is this cloud deployment model called?

Answer: B

Public Cloud

59. When assets are provided by the cloud service provider, but clouds are created and hosted privately by companies, what is this cloud deployment model called?

Answer: D

Private Cloud

60. When assets are shared by companies bound by an agreement and maintenance responsibilities are also shared, what is this cloud deployment model called?

Answer: C

Community Cloud

61. When there is a combination of two or more clouds, what is this cloud deployment model called?

Answer: B

Hybrid Cloud

62. What is the name of the file that stores the user account information in UNIX and LINUX operating systems?

Answer: A

/etc/passwd

63. When a file is accessible only by the administrator and stores the encrypted passwords of user accounts in UNIX and LINUX operating systems, what is this file called?

Answer: C

/etc/shadow

64. When a combination of processes work together to ensure that specific system/database/network is always available, what is this technique called?

Answer: C

High Availability

65. When a standard of best practices for IT processes like incident and problem management, IT financial management, etc. is adopted, what is this framework called?

Answer: D

ITIL

66. When a system allows diverse levels of data to be processed and makes access decisions as per the users' security clearances, what is this technique called?

Answer: D

Multilevel Security

16

Answers To Security Assessment and Testing

1. What is the practice of assessing information security controls of an organization and verifying their compliance with information security standards called?
   Answer: C

   Security audit

2. When a chronological record of events and documentary evidence related to the user activities is maintained, what is this technique called?
   Answer: A

   Audit logging

3. What is the open source penetration tool that automates the execution of attacks and saves testers time by removing many lengthy steps involved, called?
   Answer: A

   Metasploit

4. What is the method of evaluating software tests by modifying a program and analyzing the difference between the original and the mutated program versions called?
   Answer: B

Mutation testing

5. When a process determines the OS used by a host of network, what is the technique called?
   Answer: D

   OS fingerprinting

6. What is the testing method that is used to verify that the change has had an expected effect after the implementation of an update/change in a software called?
   Answer: D

   Non-regression testing (NRT)

7. What is the type of scanning that sends a single packet to each scanned port with the SYN flag set, indicating a request for a new connection called?
   Answer: B

   TCP SYN Scanning

8. What is the type of scanning that opens a full connection to the remote system on the specified port called?
   Answer: A

   TCP Connect Scanning

9. What is the type of scanning that sends a packet to each scanned port with the ACK flag set, indicating that it is part of an open connection called?
Answer: C

TCP ACK Scanning

10. When an attacker alters normal PHP URLs and variables to remotely include and execute malicious content, what is this web vulnerability called?
Answer: C

PHP Remote File Inclusion (RFI)

11. When an attacker installs and runs a backdoor and exploits username/passwords left behind in the code by programmers, what is this web vulnerability called?
Answer: C

Hard-coded Credentials

12. Which of the following is a phase of Code Review?
Answer: A

Inspection